D1074634

TEXAS MEN

Big Guns, Rising Stars & Cowboys

TEXAS MEN

BIG GUNS, RISING STARS & COWBOYS

✕

MARTANA

Foreword by Larry Hagman

CF Ranch Publishing, Fort Worth, Texas

COPYRIGHT © 2000 BY RANCH TEXAS ENTERTAINMENT, LTD.

FOREWORD © 2000 BY LARRY HAGMAN

All rights reserved. No part of this book may be reproduced
or transmitted in any form or by any means, electronic or
mechanical, including photocopying, recording, or by any information storage or retrieval system, except brief excerpts for the
purpose of review, without written permission of the publisher.

CF RANCH PUBLISHING
Ranch Texas Entertainment, LTD.
4800 Bryant Irvin Court
Fort Worth, Texas 75601
www.txmen.com

DISTRIBUTED BY TEN SPEED PRESS
P.O. BOX 7123
Berkeley, California 94707
www.tenspeed.com

Distributed in Australia by Simon and Schuster Australia, in
Canada by Ten Speed Press Canada, in New Zealand by
Southern Publishers Group, in South Africa by Real Books, in
Southeast Asia by Berkeley Books, and in the United Kingdom
and Europe by Airlift Book Company.

Printed in Hong Kong

Design by Matt Hahn, ThinkDesign, Buellton, California

LIBRARY OF CONGRESS CATALOGING–IN–PUBLICATION DATA

Martana, date.
        Texas men : big guns, rising stars & cowboys /
Martana ; foreword by Larry Hagman ; photography by Texas
photographers.
        p. cm.

I S B N   0-9616868-1-2 (alk. paper)

1.   Texas——Biography. I. Title

CT262 .m29 2000
920.0764—dc21
[B]

        00-023650

First Printing, 2000

1 2 3 4 5 6 7 8 9 10 — 04 03 02 01 00

Dedicated to My Mother

For returning home
to Texas
just in time,
so I would be born
a 6th generation
Texan!

FOREWORD

Everybody knows "everything's bigger in Texas." As a native from Fort Worth, I was lucky to land the ultimate role—as the Texas Man people love to hate! The villainous TV legend "J. R. Ewing," of the 80s television show *Dallas*, was the quintessential Texas Man in the eyes of the world. Don't we all own oil wells, live on sprawling ranches, wear boots and cowboy hats, and make million-dollar deals every Friday? ✷ *Texas Men* proves that Texas is more than just an image—and that's why I am honored to introduce the legends and personalities featured here. Texas has much more to showcase than the oil industry—though that plays an important part in the Lone Star State's past. Now, Texas is a diverse land of Internet geniuses, legal eagles, banking barons and high-tech trailblazers. It's a new frontier of entrepreneurs and restaurateurs. It's a country all its own. ✷ As I page through *Texas Men*, I recognize many of the men featured. Reading the "Tall Texas Tales" made me laugh because I've heard some of these tales before! As a matter of fact, I could tell a little tale about the first time I met Martana. I was in the lobby of the Crescent Court Hotel when this long, tall Texas woman rushed in apologizing for being late. Her car had just caught fire on the freeway, but instead of missing our meeting, she walked a mile in her boots down the sweltering hot Texas highway as soon as the fire trucks arrived at the scene. Brushing off her brow, she held out a hand and introduced me to the *Texas Men* project. Now that's what I call true Texas grit. ✷ I tip my hat to the men in this book—and I am proud to be one of them. Open *Texas Men* and meet the legends of Texas.

Larry Hagman

INTRODUCTION

Texas Men are one of a kind. They're brash and beautiful, wily and charming, sexy and sincere. They're as comfortable in button-down shirts and business suits as they are in blue jeans and cowboy boots. They're headstrong, determined and stubborn—but they're always gentlemen. They open doors for women, and they call their mamas "ma'am." ★ The men in this book are the new Texas legends; they are the heroes future generations will remember. They are CEOs, chefs and billionaires; politicians, Internet moguls and artists; sports heroes, ranchers and movie stars. They hail from towns like Comfort, Dallas, Art and El Paso. These men are right here in Texas! They embody the courage and independence of this once-sovereign republic, and their unstoppable spirit will shepherd the Lone Star State into the future. ★ Why did I write this book? Everywhere I travel people stop me on the street to ask if I'm from Texas. Perhaps it's my blonde hair, or my strong Texas accent or the lizard boots I like to wear. Perhaps it's a combination of all three—people can spot a Texan seven coffee shops away. They want to know if Texas is really like *Dallas*, the blockbuster television show from the 1980s (which, incidentally, many people still watch!). Do I live on a ranch and get around town on horseback? Am I rich from the oil wells I own? Do I have a conniving uncle named J.R.? This insatiable fascination with Texas is why I wrote this book: to show people around the world that the real men of Texas are more than just images they've see on television shows and in old Western movies. Real Texas Men are rugged, handsome, wealthy and humble—and although J.R. doesn't really live at Southfork, and all Texans don't wear ten-gallon hats, there are characters in Texas more engaging than any television producer could create. ★ When people ask me how I selected the men for the book, I tell them, "It was a tough job, but somebody had to do it!" I wanted to include men who best represent the state of Texas, and I knew that would mean finding a combination of famous, infamous, and not-so-well-known men. I wanted this book to showcase the immense landscape of personalities that Texas has to offer. ★ Everyone from my expert advisory board to my mechanic gave me suggestions about who should be included. I collected names written on napkins, match books, Post-it notes, and business cards, and with a long list of notable men who have accomplished the extraordinary, I sat down to make the final list. Those featured are certainly not the only great men in Texas (I'd have to produce many more books to capture all of Texas' intriguing characters), but these men do stand out from the rest, if only for the deep friendships and respect they cultivate, and the civic generosity they display. ★ While writing this book I met true heroes, men who have saved lives, raised millions of dollars to help others, and unselfishly shared their wisdom and creativity with the world. I traveled to their personal offices, ranches, restaurants, rodeo arenas and Indian reservations to capture their personalities and to photograph them in their element. ★ In true Texas style, my introduction to rancher Al Micallef took place in a helicopter five thousand feet above the ground. We toured his ranch in Alpine by air, then sat down to lunch prepared by the chef from Reata restaurant in Fort Worth, who had been flown in just for this occasion to fix us lunch! And I never dreamed I'd have the opportunity to spend the day with Chuck Norris and his crew on the set of *Walker, Texas Ranger*. I shouldn't have been surprised by the incredible experiences I encountered while compiling this book because Texas Men do everything in a big way. But for all their show, they remain good-hearted, kind and authentic people. ★ I'm proud to say that the jacket on this book is also authentic—real Texas, through and through. A pair of Al Micallef's chaps were photographed to create the leather background; the engraved silver letters of the title and my silver nameplate were designed and etched by Shannon Morrow of Big Bend Saddlery in Alpine; and the branded state of Texas was seared into a pair of leather chaps with a red-hot branding iron by the cowboys of CF Ranch. ✶ The jacket photo tells a tale as well. The three pairs of boots represent the "Big Guns, Rising Stars & Cowboys" of the title. "Big Guns" would never be caught in dusty boots—their boots always have a high shine. They are heroes and legends, accomplished in their endeavors. "Rising Stars" are trailblazers and trail bosses—future legends. Our "Rising

Star" is wearing stovetop boots—a statement of confidence with a little flash and dash. "Cowboys" wear well-worn boots, chaps and spurs, of course. They are working cowboys, urban cowboys, high-tech cowboys and all-around cowboys. In order of appearance, the boots on the cover are modeled by Texas Men Joe T. Lancarte, Steve Murrin and Jim Calhoun, Jr. ✶ Even the typestyle used for each man's "Favorite Texas Saying" represents the font from an original Republic of Texas court document from the 1800s I discovered while researching my great-great-grandfather's history. ✶ It was important to me to document the legacy of Texas, and I am proud to spotlight the Texas Men who have made the Lone Star State what it is today. I hope this book will give people a deeper understanding of what it means to be a Texan, and will prove that a country boy with a slow drawl and dusty boots can grow up to change the world with a little hard work and a dream. If reading this book makes people want to come to Texas—well then, I've done my job.

ACKNOWLEDGMENTS

This book represents a passion of mine: Texas. It has taken more than two years to research and compile this list of great men, to take their photographs and to write their stories. I appreciate the people who worked on this book—those who inspired me, instructed me, and helped me create *Texas Men*—more than you'll ever know. You are my heroes and heroines. ⋆ My applause to Texas photographers Ray Payne, Fran Reisner, Mikel Wixson, and all the other photographers whose winning photographs capture the men and their passions. As I look back through the pages of this book, I am amazed at how well the images bring to life the heart and soul of these Texas Men. I would like to thank Lou George of BWC Photo Imaging for processing; Peter Chestnut for kicking off our project; Cliff Smith of Kodak Professional for providing the film which let Texas' true colors shine. Thanks to Debbie Jackson for her superior ability to keep track of all the images and to Shelly Johnson for keeping these Texas boys' colors true. ⋆ Hats off to Al Micallef, who believed in the project from the start and whose generous participation and commitment to producing the book is deeply appreciated; and to his outstanding crew at JMK International: Mike Evans; Cathy Snoddy, my whole-hearted thanks for your warmth, guidance and help in keeping everything running smoothly; Sue Stephenson; T. J. Jones and Dawn Wood—a million thanks! ⋆ My special thanks to everyone at Ten Speed, champions of this vast project: Dennis Hayes, Phil Wood and Jo Ann Deck, for generously sharing their knowledge of the book business, and Julie Bennett, queen of editing. Cheers to Matt Hahn of ThinkDesign, who is a wellspring of creativity; he understood my vision of "Texas elegance" and created a museum-quality design that I am very proud of. Thanks to Asia Pacific for your guidance through the printing process; editor Macy Jaggers for her unerring rules of punctuation and style; and Sally Rodgers for editing and re-editing the perfect profile layout. ⋆ My respect and ovation for the tireless efforts and dedication of the *Texas Men* team: my advisory board for their expertise; Laurel Barrett, for her constant encouragement and fantastic marketing skills; Andrea Chestnut, for keeping the office running during this crazy time; Brooke Malouf, for her entertaining interviews and writing collaborations; Ivan Martinez; Kathy Seery; Tauma Wiggins (aka Tomahawk), for her ability to track down any Texas man for a profile; and to all the other people who worked in the *Texas Men* office. Bravo to the University of Dallas MBA Capstone class for their marketing research report, and to the assistants of the Texas Men—you are saints for prodding, pleading and faxing all the material for their pages— bless you! ⋆ A big hug to all of the Texas Twenty Sponsors—are you ready to have some fun? ⋆ My adoration and deep appreciation to friends, old and new, who supported me in this accomplishment: my long-time fan, Robert Bennett, for always being there when I needed him, and whose friendship, generous help and enthusiasm for this project will always be treasured; Al G. Hill, Jr., for believing in my vision when it was only an idea, and taking a leap of faith in this project—his generous support and constant encouragement will always be remembered; Bob Hopkins, for his amazing energy and ideas; Lester Levy, Jr., for buying the first table at the Lone Star Night event and being a great supporter; and to all the Texans I've met along the way who contributed names and ideas, introduced me to their friends and offered their hospitality to the *Texas Men* team throughout this project. ⋆ A BIG Texas thank you to all the women of the Lone Star State for taking care of our Texas Men, and my heartfelt thanks to Dr. Red Duke, who was too busy saving lives to make it into this book, but whose Hermann Hospital Life Flight Helicopter Program saved the life of one of our Texas Men, Mills Duncan. ⋆ Most of all, my love, gratefulness and remembrance to the five generations of women before me, for teaching me what it means to be a Texas woman. Observing the strength and kindness they share with people in everyday life has been a great lesson. Thank you for showing me that I can do anything I set my mind to. ⋆ If only this book were as big as Texas, I could thank all of the people who whole-heartedly gave their time and energy to help make this book a reality!

Live Big . . . Martana Joy

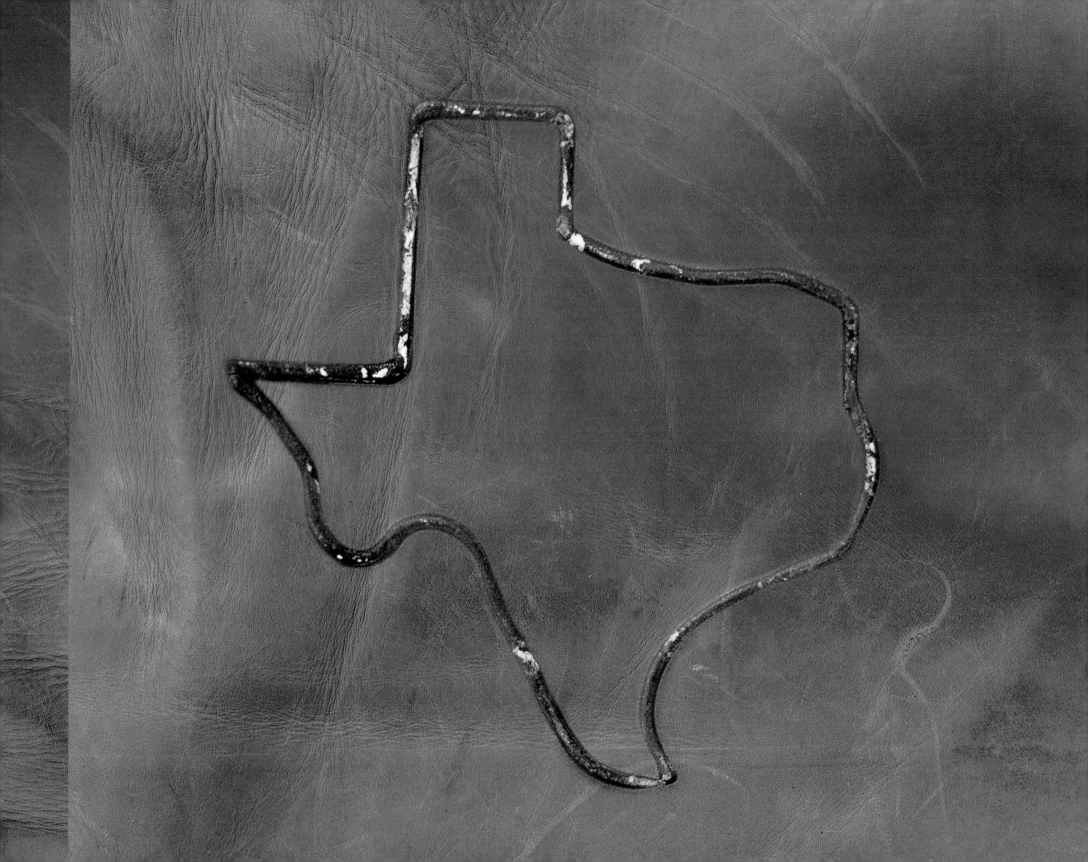

TABLE OF CONTENTS

JAY BOY ADAMS
KING OF THE ROAD

TOURED THE SUMMER OF '99 PERFORMING ON THE BILL OF THE GEORGE STRAIT COUNTRY MUSIC FESTIVAL!

My Texas post is: Founder, Roadhouse Transportation. We cater to the transportation needs of entertainers with decked-out tour buses. We have hauled stars from ZZ Top to Celine Dion to the Governor of Texas!

I was born & raised in: Born in Fort Worth, TX and raised in Colorado City, TX.

I hang my hat in: Waring, TX, on a ranch with the Guadalupe river running through it.

I came into this world on: December 8,1949 at sunrise, 6:30 a.m. I've been rising early ever since.

I'm a real cowboy because: Bob Macy said so!

If you run into my friend Bill Worrell: Ask him about the time the Reese's candy bar wrapper "accidentally" blew out of my hand. Bill was the scoutmaster and I was one of the scouts in the back of his 1953 Chevy pick-up truck. He pulled over about a mile later and sent me back for the wrapper. I returned with the first candy wrapper I saw in the ditch, which happened to be a Baby Routh but apparently Worrell knew I had been eating a Reese's and he sent me back. I found that wrapper and haven't littered a Reese's since.

If you walked a mile in my boots: You'd have the time of your life!

I love Texas because: There's no place like it. It's the finest place on earth.

"If I tell you a rooster can pull a

"He and his company have hauled everyone from . . . ZZ TOP . . . [to] The Dallas Cowboys . . . [to] the Governor of Texas . . ."

I asked J.W. Williams to write my "Tall Texas Tale" because:

More than anyone, J.W. has been down this road with me. He's walked many of the same miles that I have and because of this he knows my journey better than anyone other than myself.

freight train—you better hook him up."

— Jay's Favorite Texas Saying

Lone Wolf Management Company®

Dear Martana,

Almost thirty years ago, I met a young musician in the University Center at Texas Tech University in Lubbock. Little did I know at the time the effect that introduction would have on my life. This fellow carried himself like a man who knew exactly where he was going and had a very good idea of how to get there in a manner that fit his style. And style he had. At a time when hair past your shoulders and a full beard were grounds to have your rear end whipped in West Texas; this young fellow was fearless. Weighing in at all of 110 pounds soaking wet, he could stare down the biggest redneck that foolishly attempted to block his way. I will never cease to chuckle at some of the confrontations we have withstood together over the last three decades. Whether he was talking a drunken club owner into actually paying him after he had just finished playing 4-hour sets, or insisting that a client actually pay him for the services he had just provided, he always seemed to have the business savvy and people skills to walk away from each situation a winner.

Besides possessing good tracking and hunting skills, he is probably the best cook the West has ever produced, with his skill over a fire closing on legendary. Definitely a chuck-wagon cook in former life, Jay spends his happiest moments these days, when not with his family, staring down a camp fire until the coals are just right for cooking the steaks for which he has become so famous. Our most pleasant recent memories have been tracking Whitetail deer from the Hill Country to Canada or Dove Hunts in South Texas and the pay-off always is the meal after the day's work. Legend has it that he has been known to even empty his gun at a 12-point decoy!

Born of proud West Texas traditions and of parents, who were both bigger than life figures to all that met them, this son of Mitchell, County was destined for great things. In his life he has met and married the love of his life, witnessed the birth of his two precious children and enjoyed two successful careers, first as an entertainer performing to hundreds of thousands of people all across North America. His quest for stardom has brought him from the dingy dives of Dallas to the jewel in the crown of performing theaters, Carnegie Hall in New York. It brought him from rodeo barns in Iowa to the University of Texas Memorial Stadium for the infamous ZZ TOP's Rompin' Stompin' Barn Dance and Bar B Que, where he opened for an audience of 80,000. And most recently appearing with George Strait on the 1999 Stadium Tour and with Lee Roy Parnell at Lee Roy's Fan Fair gig in Nashville.

After pursuing the elusive glamour and glitter of the touring life as an artist, this young visionary knew he had discovered the better mousetrap. Applying all the experience of the artist to a then burgeoning transportation industry catering to the entertainment industry, Jay Boy began catering to the needs of entertainers. He founded Roadhouse Transportation and became "King of the Road." There is nothing like first-hand experience, especially when you have to travel for a living. His unique perspective of the needs of a very specialized and particular clientele has served him well. He and his company have hauled everyone from Shania Twain to Bruce Springsteen, the "Artist" who can't remember his name (Prince), to ZZ TOP, Clint Black to Boyz to Men, Dire Straits to Billy Joel. The list goes on to include Celine Dion, The Dallas Cowboys, Lee Roy Parnell who I think is Jay's twin brother from different parents, the Governor of Texas, and the First Lady of the United States. Obviously, he has found another niche.

The most amazing part of all this is that he has managed to remain the same soulful man of character I met out on the Caprock so long ago. I'm proud to be among his friends.

Sincerely,

J.W. Williams

J. W. Williams

P.O. BOX 163690 · AUSTIN, TEXAS 78716 · (512) 314-WOLF · FAX (512) 314-9650
E-MAIL: info@lone-wolf.com

JOHN ADAMS
ROUGH CREEK LODGE

DEVELOPED & SOLD THREE SUCCESSFUL PHARMACEUTICAL COMPANIES

My Texas post is: Chairman of the Board, Adams Laboratories; and Owner, Rough Creek Lodge, Executive Retreat & Conference Center, in Glen Rose, TX. But on the weekends you can find me on the deck of my house at Chalk Mountain Ranch, sippin' a scotch or fishin' at the lodge.

I came into this world on: November 17, 1936—with empty pockets.

I hang my hat in: Colleyville, TX—next door to Cowtown.

I'm a real cowboy because: I'm most at home when my boots touch the ground at the ranch or at the lodge.

If you run into my friend Ed Hiebert ask him about the time: He built a fan out of an airplane propeller to cool our warehouse. He nearly blew all our product off the shelf!

If you walked a mile in my boots: You'd be quail hunting at Rough Creek Lodge.

I love Texas because: The people and the place have provided exceptional opportunities and lasting relationships for my family and me. In my view, Texas is the best place to accomplish and enjoy this Texas lifestyle!

"Tougher than the back wall of a Texas Shooting Gallery."

— John's Favorite Texas Saying

THOMPSON & KNIGHT
L.L.P.
ATTORNEYS AND COUNSELORS

1700 PACIFIC AVENUE • SUITE 3300
DALLAS, TEXAS 75201-4693
(214) 969-1700
FAX (214) 969-1751
www.tklaw.com

AUSTIN
DALLAS
FORT WORTH
HOUSTON
MONTERREY, MEXICO

DIRECT DIAL:

(214) 969-1354
E-Mail: burfords@tklaw.com

June 29, 2000

Dear Martana:

A little over thirty years ago this summer, as a green young lawyer fresh out of law school, my boss at the law firm dispatched me to the mid-cities area between Dallas and Fort Worth under orders to handle the legal affairs for some guy in the pharmaceutical business that went by the name of "John Quincy Adams, Sr." This somewhat imposing gentleman came on stronger than a bowl of green Mexican chilies. He soon toughened me up to the ways of the business world, and not only have I been his lawyer for the last thirty or so years, we have become very close friends and hunting partners.

"J.Q.", as he is known in Texas circles, is not your basic mild mannered, quiet and refined chief executive officer. In fact, I would describe his basic philosophy of life as "anything worth doing is worth overdoing". J.Q. has started, developed, and successfully sold three companies over the last thirty years and is working on number four right now! Nobody ever told him that he did not have to keep working every day, so he just gets up every morning and honestly believes that he needs to skin a rabbit every day for dinner. I believe this trait is what has made J.Q. a major success in both business and in life.

A typical example of his "gather no moss" lifestyle is the time we decided he needed to have some fun instead of working all the time. We gave him a cheap shotgun and an over-the-hill, mangy-looking hunting dog. In typical "J.Q." fashion, he now owns some of the world's finest shotguns and reigns over a world class hunting lodge on 11,000 acres southwest of Fort Worth with one of the world's finest chefs, forty Texas chic-style guest rooms and the President George Bush Suite in which J.Q. resides while there. Rough Creek Lodge, Adams' "hobby", maintains over thirty-five of the finest hunting dogs in the State of Texas, upland bird hunting for quail, chukar, Hungarian partridge and mallards, not to mention one of his favorite activities, a European pheasant shooting course on a part of the ranch specially built for such purpose. The hundred-acre lake and other recreational facilities including horseback riding, mountain biking and tennis are simply incidentals to J.Q.

Although as a business man, John Quincy Adams is tougher than the back wall of a Texas shooting gallery and one Texas-tough negotiator, he has given back to the community through charitable donations, conservation of land and animals in Texas and the creation of a scholarship at Vanderbilt University. In my estimation, "J.Q." is a true Texas legend, and I am proud to be among his colleagues and friends.

Sincerely,

Sam

Sam P. Burford, Jr.

SPB:dc

08234 00001 Dallas 1161586.1

" ... he just gets up every morning and honestly believes that he needs to skin a rabbit every day for dinner."

I asked Sam Burford to write my "Tall Texas Tale" because: *We have worked and played together for 30 years. We know how to make acquisitions and divestitures fun!*

ED AULER
WINEMAKER, FALL CREEK VINEYARDS

WON OVER 400 MEDALS IN STATE, NATIONAL & INTERNATIONAL WINE COMPETITIONS

My Texas post is: Owner and Winemaker, Fall Creek Vineyards, Llano County, with a corporate office in Austin, TX.

I came into this world on: July 28, 1945—a great year for wine!

I was born & raised in: Austin, TX, when it was a sleepy, "low-tech" town on the edge of the Hill Country.

I hang my hat in: Austin and points west in the Hill Country, as well as Big Bend.

I'm a real cowboy because: I have cattle operations in 5 counties.

If you run into my friend Bob Clement ask him about the: Bull I sold him and our escapades in capturing that bull over the next three months, as the bull took a self-guided tour through the Texas Hill Country.

If you walked a mile in my boots: You'd be in lots of places where your cell phone wouldn't work.

I love Texas because: No place else is even a contender!

"It's not how long you've been here, it's what you did after you got here."

— Ed's Favorite Texas Saying

CafeAnnie

To the audience:

Ed Auler knows all the words — not just a couple of verses
But all the verses and all the words:

*Out in the West Texas Town of El Paso
I fell in love with a Mexican Girl . . .*

Not like me, who's good for only a line or two here and there,
Or like Dean Fearing, who can make up the words as he goes along:
No — Ed knows all the words.

*Cradled by two loving arms that I'd die for
One little kiss and Felina good-bye.*

Dean and I would tune him up and say, "Hey Ed, how about *Ghost Riders!*"
And Ed would strum a little while just staring straight ahead,
Out over his vineyards all in neat rows like a ready audience,
And then, without even an "OK boys - a one, two, three . . ."
He'd break right into it:

*An old cowpoke went riding out one dark and windy day
Upon a ridge he rested as he went along his way . . .*

And Dean and I, all charged up on Ed's fine red wine
Would hang on the rhythmic movement of Ed's fingers,
Catching as catch can the chord changes, while trying to add
A little C & W here, a couple of guitar tricks there,
But always aiming to chime in on the chorus:

*Yippie-i-ay . . . Yippie-i-ooooo
Ghost riders in the sky.*

Yeah - out under the Texas stars in a cool evening breeze
With glasses of cool red wine, we'd work our way through
Songs that seem to ignore the weathering hand of time;
And the audience of vines, always standing in respectful ovation,
Would give us a rustle of applause. Then after a smiling respite
Of sipping and tuning, we'd call out another one:
"Hey Ed, how about *Big Iron* . . . And Ed would quietly strum,
Reading the vineyards for a sign until without fail, he'd break right into it -

*To the town of Aqua Fria road a stranger one fine day
Hardly spoke to folks around him, didn't have too much to say
No one dared to ask his business, no one dared to make a slip
For the stranger there among them had a Big Iron on his hip,
. . . Big Iron his hip.*

Only Ed could do it - because Ed Auler knows all the words.

Regards,

Robert Del Grande

1728 POST OAK BOULEVARD • HOUSTON, TX 77056 • 713.840.1111 • FAX 713.840.1558 • www.cafe-annie.com

An Affiliate of Schiller Del Grande ✳ Restaurant Group

I asked Robert Del Grande to write my "Tall Texas Tale" because: *He has supported our Fall Creek wines from the beginning, and he, Dean Fearing and I picked and wailed Texas songs under the name "Barbed Wires."*

"Not like me..."
"Or like Dean Fearing..."
"No—Ed knows all the words."

JOHN AYCOCK
TEXAS RANGER

"There are many tales on John, including one we will never let him live down."

I asked Captain Bob Mitchell and Captain Joe Wilie to write my "Tall Texas Tale" because:
They are and always have been my heroes.

TEXAS DEPARTMENT OF PUBLIC SAFETY
PO BOX 4087   AUSTIN TX 78773-0001
TEXAS RANGERS

DUDLEY M. THOMAS
DIRECTOR

THOMAS A. DAVIS, JR.
ASST. DIRECTOR

COMMISSION
JAMES B. FRANCIS, JR.
CHAIRMAN
ROBERT B. HOLT
M. COLLEEN McHUGH
COMMISSIONERS

Dear Martana,

John Aycock is a great American and one of the finest Texans we have known. Besides being a highly decorated Vietnam veteran, he is the only man in the history of the Texas Department of Public Safety to win two Medals of Valor, the highest award given by that department. It was an honor and privilege to have served as his commanding officers in the Texas Rangers for many years.

But we also know John as a very caring person and have spent many an hour talking with him about things that most people never know a Ranger or any law enforcement officer can experience after an especially traumatic investigation. John is always willing to go the old proverbial "extra mile" to make sure everyone involved got a "fair shake" because he really cares. His heart is as big as his hat.

There are many tales on John, including one we will never let him live down. For many years during deer hunting season John would put together a hunt for law enforcement officers, judges and prosecutors on the ranch of one of his friends in Bell County. One year in the early morning hours, John called all the hunters together to tell us the ranch had several exotic animals and we were to be careful to not shoot any of them.

At noon we were picked up from our hunting stands and brought to the ranch house for lunch. It was there that we learned one of the finest exotic animals on the ranch had been killed. You guessed it. None other than Texas Ranger John Aycock, who had lectured us so hard that morning, was the red-faced culprit. He will never hear the end of this deer hunt!

The Texas Rangers have existed since 1823. Stephen F. Austin, the Father of Texas, appointed ten men to range between certain rivers to scout the movement of Indians and to warn the settlers of their location. The Texas Rangers of today still protect the citizens of Texas. Texans can sleep well at night knowing that Texas Rangers like John Aycock are out there watching out for their welfare.

So we are proud to be able to put in our two cents worth about John Aycock (the other 98 cents worth is just between him and us) for your book, and to let the citizens of Texas know there are still people like Ranger John Aycock out there to protect and serve and truly CARE.

Sincerely,

Captain Bob Mitchell

Captain Joe Wilie

COURTESY – SERVICE - PROTECTION

ACHIEVING A LIFELONG DREAM OF BECOMING A TEXAS RANGER, WINNING 2 MEDALS OF VALOR & SURVIVING ALL OF IT!

My Texas post is: Texas Rangers, Company "F."

I came into this world on: The night that I was born—"Nuff said."

I was born & raised in: The western part of Texas.

I hang my hat in: The central and southern part of Texas.

I'm a real cowboy because: I was born one and like it.

If you run into my friends George Strait and Roy Cooper ask them about: Our three-horse race with a one-horse winner at the Cheyenne Frontier Days Rodeo in Wyoming. By the time George picked up my glasses, my hat, made sure I hadn't broken my neck and Roy quit laughing—it was clear we had a winner. Heck, I was the only one who'd even left the starting line!

If you run into my other friends Ranger Fred Cummings and Captain Joe Wilie ask them about the time: My white cowdog W.D. tricked me into buying her a full drive-thru meal! As we were gettin' in my state car to go grab a Whataburger, W.D. jumped into my passenger seat and wouldn't budge. Then, at the drive-thru she wouldn't stop barking till I ordered her a burger and fries. Would you believe she even wanted dessert after all that!

If you walked a mile in my boots: You would cover ground pretty quickly!

I love Texas because: Of the wide open spaces, the stars in the sky that you can touch and that take your heart away, and the friendly people wherever you go. There is no place in this world I've ever found that even comes close to Texas.

"God Bless Texas!"

— John's Favorite Texas Saying

JERRY BAILEY
"THE GENERAL," ALL-STAR JOCKEY

WINNER OF 2 KENTUCKY DERBIES, 2 PREAKNESSES & 1 BELMONT STAKES

My Texas post is: Deep in the saddle.

I came into this world on: August 29, 1957—on a wing and a prayer.

I was born in Dallas and raised in: El Paso—where it's hot, dusty and windy . . . even the horses think so!

I'm a real cowboy because: I ride at least three horses everyday.

If you walked a mile in my boots: You'd weigh less than 110 pounds!

I love Texas because: That's where I got my start racing horses.

"You're responsible for the effort, not the outcome."

— Jerry's Favorite Texas Saying

"Here's my nomination of a fabulously successful rider and part-time race track comedian— Jerry Bailey."

I asked Norm Hitzges to write my "Tall Texas Tale" because:

He's the only person in Texas who will still talk to me!

LONE STAR PARK
at Grand Prairie

Dear Martana,

The Hall of Fame for humor boasts the names of funny men like Jackie Gleason, Robin Williams, Richard Pryor and Uncle Miltie. Throw Archie Bunker in there too. But a jockey? Here's my nomination of a fabulously successful rider and part-time race track comedian—Jerry Bailey. Anyone can yuck it up when they're winning, but some of Bailey's best lines came after losses.

Years ago the Dallas-born Bailey was atop a hot Kentucky Derby contender named Technology in a key prep race for the Derby. The thing ran like it had been sired by a poodle. Afterward, a disappointed Bailey gave the racing world a description of the trip he'd just taken that would have made the writers for *Saturday Night Live* proud. Said Bailey: "We were going along okay when it came time for us to make a move on the leaders. Then, all-of-a-sudden, the holes were moving faster than we were." What a perfect picture!

And he's not afraid to tell jokes on himself. In the early 80s, after a particularly long night, Bailey reported to the track at the crack of dawn to work out an animal at the special request of trainer Sid Waters. For some reason the horse ran like it was pulling a wagon. Bailey, miffed that he'd shortened a perfectly good night's sleep to exercise such a hound, barked at trainer Waters: "You got me up early to work a piece of BLEEP like this?" Why does Bailey still recall that morning nearly two decades later? Because that "piece of BLEEP" named Slew O' Gold went on to win an astounding $3.5 million as a multiple graded stakes winner.

But should Bailey fall a bit short of induction into the "Comedy Hall of Fame," his place in racing is already assured. That Hall welcomed him in 1995 at age 38. So, just where does this Texas riding legend rank on the list of the best thoroughbred jockeys of all-time? First? Second? (Just behind fellow Texan, Bill Shoemaker?) Third? Fifth? Who cares! How many people will ever be able to say, as Bailey can that whatever their chosen field of achievement, they're unquestionably amongst the best ever? First introduced to racing at age 11 by his Texas dentist father James Bailey, Jerry was already riding quarter horse match race winners. At age 17 his first ever thoroughbred ride came aboard a runner named Fetch. He won. He's just kept on winning. You want gaudy numbers? I'll "Fetch 'em" for you:

- Top 10 in purses, an outrageous 11 years in a row (1989-99) including leading the world in three of those years.
- Kentucky Derbies won? Two.
- Breeders Cup Classics? Four.
- Eclipse Awards as the planet's best rider? Three.
- Belmont Stakes, Preakness, the $4 million Dubai World Cup? Bailey's been there and done them.
- He rode the legendary Cigar to an all-time record tying 16 straight victories.
- Now, he's passing 5000 winners ridden and $200,000,000 in purses earned.

So whether it's his "gallows humor" about losing rides or the thousands of smiles he's flashed while getting his picture taken in the winners circle, Jerry Bailey and those smart enough to back him at the pari-mutuel windows just keep laughing all the way to the bank.

Norm Hitzges

Norm Hitzges

1000 LONE STAR PARKWAY ★ GRAND PRAIRIE, TEXAS 75050 ★ PHONE (972) 263-7223 ★ FAX (972) 262-5622 ★ *www.lonestarpark.com*

JOHN PAUL BATISTE
TEXAS COMMISSION ON THE ARTS

JOCELYN L. STRAUS

Dear Martana,

He runs a mile a minute! In fact, running track is how this Tall Texas man won his college scholarship. John Paul Batiste is a rare individual who is extraordinarily talented in so many different areas.

He had aspirations of being a minister and studied philosophy and theology. He earned a BA in History and Literature from Texas College in Tyler, followed by studies at Texas A&M in Arts Administration and Early Childhood Development at Texas Southern University. John Paul was the Assistant Director for Training and Administration for the Dallas Head Start programs and served as Community Relations Director for the University of Houston's Bilingual/Multicultural Educational Television program.

We Texans should celebrate 1973 when John Paul joined the Texas Commission on the Arts as one of three artists in a pilot Humanities project funded by the Moody Foundation titled "T for Texas." He was the singer-songwriter in the group, which toured 13 Texas communities.

This Tall Texan was now an established Poet in Residence and Education Consultant to the Texas Commission on the Arts. For seven years the TCA benefited from his vision, his expertise and his energy. John Paul left the Texas Commission on the Arts in 1981 to become the Supervisor of Financial Services and later, Assistant Director of the Dallas City Arts program. His leadership helped build a significant number of neighborhood cultural facilities in Dallas.

In 1981, I was appointed to the Texas Commission on the Arts for a six-year term by Governor Clements. 1983 was a banner year for me and for the TCA as John Paul assumed the role of Director of Programs/Assistant Director and was responsible for restructuring the agency.

The finest year for the arts in Texas was 1988 when John Paul became the Executive Director of the Texas Commission on the Arts. As we enter a new century, we should salute this terrific Tall Texan, who has the longest and most productive tenure as Director of the TCA and is the most passionate advocate for the arts.

A few years ago I invited John Paul to be the presenter of an award I was to receive. As coffee was being served and many in the group were nodding off, John Paul began his incredible poetic composition, which brought the house down. People are still asking when the tall Texas storyteller is coming back.

John Paul Batiste -- published poet, administrator, consultant, executive director, singer, songwriter, panelist, public speaker, board member, husband and father. He has and continues to influence and inspire everyone he meets.

It is with great Texas pride that I add my name to the long list of friends who admire the spirit, dedication and devotion that he expresses as everyday examples of excellence. Hats off to a truly great man and a dear friend who is still running a mile a minute!

Joci Straus

> "People are still asking when the tall Texas storyteller is coming back."

I asked Joci Straus to write my "Tall Texas Tale" because: *Joci Straus is one of the most gracious and generous souls in Texas that I have ever known.*

Toured Texas as a Singer & Poet

My Texas post is: Executive Director of the Texas Commission on the Arts in Austin, TX. Our mission and aim is to build a receptive climate for the arts in our state and to conserve our rich and diverse heritage across generations. We serve over 2000 organizations and receive over two million requests for information and assistance a year.

I saw the light of this world on: September 3,1945—midday, just as Labor Day was kicking into high gear.

I was born & raised in: Port Arthur, TX.

I rest my cap in: Austin and Dallas, TX, `cause my children, grandchildren and family ground my heart that way.

I'm a real cowboy because: Someone has to clear what the herd leaves and grow something useful!

If you run into my friend "Honey Dripper" ask him about the time: We were busted by his mama after our Sunday "Beaumont Tale" `cause Emmit told the truth and we "stretched" a bit . . .

If you walked a mile in my boots: You would discover a tenacious soul raised in commitment, creativity, courage, faith and civility.

I love Texas because: Home is its shape, shingle and place for me. It is the place where my family, spirit, days and future are bred to breathe and breed.

"There are hungers and prizes beyond food, sport and material well-being that deserve our support and encouragement."

— John's Favorite Texas Saying

STATE OF THE ARTS

JOSEPH A. BELLINO III
BODY CARE FOR THE BEAUTIFUL

CREATED A FABULOUS BODY-CARE COMPANY CALLED "BELLINO"

My Texas post is: President, Bellino, Inc., Haute Couture Body Care, where we are making the world a more beautiful place. Oh, I'm also a trial lawyer.

I came into this world on: October 22—dancin'!

I was born & raised: Born on a mountain & raised by an old mamma lion.

I hang my hat in: Dallas, TX, but I spend some weekends in Monte Carlo.

I'm a real cowboy because: I can ride and I can shoot.

If you run into my friend Mike Powers ask him about the time I: Was riding my horse behind him during a polo game and his horse fell and flipped over on him. Mike got up more dead than alive and made the winning goal!

If you walked a mile in my boots: You would die under the pressure.

My ultimate Texas date would be: A beautiful, bold and brilliant woman, who can charm a horse as well as a country the size of Texas.

I love Texas because: The women are more beautiful here than any other place in the world!

"Everyday is an adventure."

— Joe's Favorite Texas Saying

"He danced 'til dawn, which is not unusual in Monaco —especially for 'Uncle Joe'."

I asked His Serene Highness Prince Albert of Monaco to write my "Tall Texas Tale" because: *He, myself and Mike Powers are the Good, the Bad and the Bonvivant.*

Palace of Monaco,
February 17th, 2000.

Dear Martana,

The first time I met Joe Bellino was at a formal dinner that he hosted with Mike Powers. Mike is also a Texan and owns "Le Texan" and is co-founder of Monte Carlo's Pro-celebrity golf tournament in Monaco. I learned during the evening that both Joe and I are polo enthusiasts. So we made plans for Joe and Mike to pick me up at the Crescent the next day to play polo at the Bear Creek Polo Ranch in Dallas, Texas. Joe graciously loaned me not only his horse but also a helmet, knee guards and boots. We had great fun attempting to play decent polo that day.

The next time our paths crossed was in my backyard in Monaco. Joe was dressed like an Arab Sheik at a costume ball. He danced 'til dawn, which is not unusual in Monaco —especially for "Uncle Joe".

He is often spotted "gliding" along the hallowed halls of the Hotel de Paris chatting up young damsels in distress at a sidewalk café or entertaining the locals at Sass' or Jimmy'z.

"Uncle Joe's" personality has won him many an accolade —as well as a few jealous husbands!- along the Riviera. He is a friendly guy and a true "Texas Man".

Albert de Monaco

TITO BEVERIDGE
DISTILLER. VODKA Y'ALL?

FIRST & ONLY LEGAL DISTILLERY (OF ANY KIND) IN TEXAS

My Texas post is: The distillery, Tito's Handmade Vodka in Austin, TX.

I was born & raised in: San Antonio, TX on a ranch in the Hill Country near Boerne.

I hang my hat in: Austin, TX. "God's Country" overlooking Lake Austin.

I came into this world on: September 8, 1961. It was a great day for me, but to tell the truth, I don't remember much about it!

I'm a real cowboy because: I grew up ropin' and ridin' on a cattle and horse ranch.

If you run into my friend Virgil Rosser, IV: Ask him about the night 400 of our closest "friends" showed up at his parent's home for a small gathering! He'll recall using a fire extinguisher on his younger sister's shower curtain & coaxing a jilted young man off the roof. The house survived.

If you walked a mile in my boots: You'd have a smile on your face and a bottle of vodka in your hand!

I love Texas because: The people are great, friendly & fun and there is plenty of space between them.

"Smilin' like a possum in a persimmon tree."

— Tito's Favorite Texas Saying

SOUTHWEST AIRLINES CO.

Love Field
P.O. Box 36611
Dallas, TX 75235-1611
(214) 904-4104

SOUTHWEST

June 1, 1999

Dear Martana:

Everybody knows the world would leave its orbit and crash into the sun if it were not for a plentiful supply of good vodka.

Of course if you live in undeveloped parts of the world like London, Paris, Moscow, Beijing, New York or Los Angeles any kind of vodka may do. However, in Texas it damn well better be Tito's Handmade Vodka made by Texas' first and only distillery in Austin, By God, Texas.

Tito is a real Texan, fifth generation to be exact, and to add to that he had the good sense to turn from being an oil and gas man to a vodka man just about the time the oil and gas business went South. Of course Tito had been South (South America) for quite a while before seeing the light and going for broke as an entrepreneur.

Tito's Handmade is truly sipping vodka. My personal preference is on the rocks, but you drink it any way you like. Just drink it. Tito needs the money!

My problem with Bert "Tito" Bevridge, owner, still master and champion taster, is that for many years I thought his name was Bertover.

In the late '60's when I was still living in San Antonio and putting Southwest Airlines together, we had use of a small ranch in the Hill Country in Kendell County. My older son, Rollin, Jr., had this friend from San Antonio whose family had a ranch nearby. Weekends when we were at our ranch Rollin would ask if he could have Bert over. So Bertover he became, at least as far as I was concerned, for many years. In fact much later, after I had been living in Dallas for 20 years, Rollin, Jr. was getting married and a Tito Beverage was on the invitation list for the rehearsal dinner and I had to ask who he was. Rollin, in a disgusted voice said, "Dad, that's Bertover".

As far as I am concerned real Texans make things happen and Tito certainly fits that mold having helped save the world from destruction with his vodka.

Cordially,

Rollin

Rollin W. King
Founder & First President

"Of course if you live in undeveloped parts of the world like London, Paris, Moscow . . . or Los Angeles any kind of vodka may do."

I asked Rollin King to write my "Tall Texas Tale" because: *He's a Texas legend who made his Texas-size dream come true.*

MATT BLEVINS
COLONEL BLEVINS, "THE AUCTIONEER"

" ...when ... 'Matt' Blevins gives his word on something you can bet the bank on it."

I asked Michael Luskey to write my "Tall Texas Tale" because: *I worked for Luskey's/Ryon's western wear for six years and he could tell you more about myself than I could.*

2601 North Main Street • Fort Worth, Texas 76106
800-725-RYON(7966) • 817-625-2391
fax 817-625-0457
luskeys@flash.net

www.luskeys.com

Dear Martana,

In Texas a man's word is as good as it gets. You can bet when Gains Matthew "Matt" Blevins gives his word on something you can bet the bank on it. He is as goodhearted as they come. I have depended on him many times in our business. He takes up the slack when necessary and always has a smile-nothing gets him down. He even has the physical appearance that people expect when they think about a "Texas Cowboy"-tall and "lanky" with a smile from ear to ear.

Get him started on his auctioneering and he doesn't stop. He has twice increased the live auction proceeds for the Cancer Society's Cowtown Ball held annually here in Fort Worth. One day last spring, Matt and I were carrying on our typical "BS" conversation out on the sales floor of the store with Jim Shepard ("J-Boy"), manager of the store, when J-Boy had one of his customers come walking in. It just so happened that this customer was a used heavy equipment dealer. Matt was kind of patting himself on the back about a very successful heavy equipment auction he had just completed. J-Boy's customer asked him about doing an auction for him....in Canada. You would have thought the world stopped. Matt couldn't wait on any more customers with the thought of going to Canada.

A couple of hours went by and all Matt was talking about was "Canada"! J-Boy and I took Matt back into one of the offices and explained that he was "set up". The customer wasn't a heavy equipment dealer, he wasn't from Canada and the whole thing was a set up. Matt just smiled and started talking about something else. We "got" him good. He never forgot it and still tries to "pay us back".

Matt made a good friend with J-Boy's customer-as he does with everyone he meets. He will be a wealthy man some day, whether it be monetary or from the many groups of friends he makes.

Mike Luskey

Mike Luskey

Annual Cowtown Ball's Two-Time Record Breaking Auctioneer!

My Texas post is: The great town of Roanoke, TX, but I spend most of my time behind the microphone running auctions all over the great state of Texas.

I came into this world on: What began as a gloomy Wednesday, October 4, 1967, but changed to bright and sunny when I popped out!

I was born & raised in: Roanoke, TX—a one-dog town. Don't blink your eyes or you might drive through and miss it!

I hang my hat: On my head, as I stroll through the town of Roanoke, TX.

I'm a real cowboy because: I was raised on a small horse farm, which led me to earn a Bachelor of Science degree in agriculture from Tarleton State University. At the same time I rode bulls all through my college career and in the Professional Rodeo Cowboy Association.

If you run into my friend Michael ask him about the time: He and "Jay Boy" set me up to talk to a man pretending to be interested in an equipment auction. After about 15 minutes of trying my hardest to "sell" my auction-eering capabilities to this man in front of a group of my friends, I realized it was a joke.

If you walked a mile in my boots: You would see that each step gets better and better.

My ultimate Texas date would be: To have a nice steak dinner with a kind-hearted lady while we look out towards the prairie at my herd as the sun falls behind our backs.

I love Texas because: It's pure and real.

"Do what's right, and you'll never fear no man."

— Matt's Favorite Texas Saying

RICHARD CAREY
A STONE LEGEND

EMPOWERING PEOPLE TO BE ALL THEY CAN BE

My Texas post is: Founder and President of Stone Legends, architectural cast stone elements, and Stone Magic, cast stone fireplace mantels, in Dallas, TX.

I was born & raised in: Born in Dallas and raised in Irving, home of the Dallas Cowboys.

I hang my hat in: Big "D". Home.

I came into this world: To honor my mother and father.

I'm a real cowboy because: I'll always answer your questions with a story.

If you run into my friend Karen ask her about the time I: Joined the circus for a week. We performed high-dives, entertained as clowns and for our final performance—we were lit on fire!

If you walked a mile in my boots: The people you met along the way would keep you looking forward to the next mile. Pop always said, "If you want to do it right, be ready to go the extra mile." And it seems always to be the long way around.

My ultimate Texas date would be: Just like the state—it would go on seemingly endlessly and have a wide range of topography.

I love Texas because: Texas is a great place to have a vision. And because of the people here, there are a lot of folks willing to share the vision with you. Texas natives always admire a hard worker. And from what I've seen, even the transplants soon do.

"Teach a man to fish and someday, maybe you will get invited to dinner."

— Richard's Favorite Texas Saying

AMATO RACING

44 Tunkhannock Avenue ▪ Exeter, Pennsylvania 18643
www.amatoracing.com

December 19, 1999

Dear Martana:

Ask anyone, Texans are different. They are brash, optimistic, pushy, outgoing and usually set on achieving their goals to the exclusion of all else. That would describe Richard Carey perfectly. He is a real people person, especially nice to children and just a crazy fun guy.

During the workday, his most common saying is: "If it's not about STONE, I don't want to hear it!" He eats, breathes and sleeps stone. And with this focused drive, he has taken a small, old-fashioned cast stone manufacturer and made it into the leading producer in the country, overcoming huge obstacles both inside and outside the company. He brings this same focus to everything he does from flying to golf to spring board diving. Aside for his drive for success in business, he has managed to raise four great children as a single parent (and still looking for a good woman!!) which is not an easy task, even for a Texan.

I live life in the fast lane racing at 325 mph in less than 4.5 seconds in the quarter mile always pushing the envelope to the edge without fear. When I first met Richard and decided to have him do all my trick stone for my new house, I invited him to the races. I realized then that he was a special person - aside from being a Texan. We have enjoyed many moments of fun, craziness and good friendship.

And now, Richard is trying to share what he has learned and overcome with others. He has spoken at a number of schools for children who have special needs. His message is: "If I can make it, so can you." He is a role model - showing what can be done with a good plan and plenty of hard work. He's a Texan that all children can admire.

Rising star? Big gun? Cowboy? Richard Carey is all of that and more.

Sincerely,

Joe Amato

Joe Amato

TENNECO Automotive

DYNOMAX Performance Exhaust   WALKER   RANCHO   MONROE

"He eats, breathes and sleeps stone."

I asked Joe Amato to write my "Tall Texas Tale" because: *As a five-time national champion in NHRA Top Fuel, 6000 horsepower puts him at 327 mph in less than 5 seconds, a life or death situation. But Joe slows down to make everyday people like me feel so special.*

SCOTT CASTERLINE
SPORTS AGENT

THE BEST SPORTS AGENT IN TEXAS, REPRESENTING SUPER BOWL XXX MVP LARRY BROWN, LINCOLN KENNEDY & ALBERT LEWIS

My Texas post is: Founder, President & Partner of Casterline, Lewis, Bonney & Strunk Team Sports in downtown Dallas.

I came into this world on: What my mom describes as the best day of her life, November 19. It wasn't bad for me either, although I can't remember the year.

I was born & raised in: Born in Waco, TX and raised in Rockport-Fulton, TX overlooking the Gulf of Mexico.

I hang my hat in: Dallas and Houston, TX and in many hotels across the U.S.A.

I'm a real cowboy because: I am a sixth-generation "South" Texan from Aransas County. (My family has been in Rockport-Fulton since 1845.)

If you run into my friend Judd Nelson ask him about the time: He stopped me from ending up at the Elvis Presley Marriage Chapel in Las Vegas on a whim!

If you walked a mile in my boots: I'd have to beat you up for stealing. We don't share our boots in Texas.

My ultimate Texas date would be: Dinner at the Boiling Pot and dancing at Sharkey's in Fulton, TX.

I love Texas because: It's still the last frontier. It's rich in history and wild at heart. We are raised in Texas to believe we can succeed at anything we do.

"This ain't my first rodeo."

— Scott's Favorite Texas Saying

"Too bad for me he is not a theatrical agent— or that I don't run a 4.2, 40-yard dash."

I asked Judd Nelson to write my "Tall Texas Tale" because:
He's crazier than I am. Although he's a Yankee and now lives in Hollywood, he's a pretty good old boy and a heck of a friend.

Judd Nelson

Dear Martana,

First of all, I would like to thank you for asking me to write a few words about Scott Casterline: it is indeed an honor.

I met Scott in Los Angeles a number of years ago through a mutual friend, and we immediately hit it off. I found him to be bright, ambitious, and very Texan. Remember: I am a Yankee from Maine, so I always picture Scott in cowboy boots and a ten-gallon hat.

I am a degenerate sports junkie, so I was thrilled when Scott would take the time to talk with me about his behind-the-scenes work in athletic representation. How refreshing it was to discover someone who puts his clients and their families ahead of the bottom line. Too bad for me he is not a theatrical agent - or that I don't run a 4.2, 40-yard dash.

During a trip to Dallas a number of years ago, I managed to stumble into a small "predicament." Scott was very helpful in providing me with much counsel, which went a long way toward resolving the matter. I will always be thankful.

Scott Casterline is a good man, and I am proud to be considered one of his many friends. God Bless Texas for producing him.

Sincerely,

Judd Nelson

Judd Nelson

TEXAS A&M
UNIVERSITY
COMMERCE

Dear Martana:

Some Texans are born for greatness—others just work hard to achieve it. So goes the tale of MIKE CAVENDER, of Cavender's Boot City—the largest boot seller in the world.

In elementary school, Mike was displaying entrepreneurial characteristics. He worked in the boot shop in Pittsburg, Texas, for his dad on commission. Needless to say, that didn't last long—his dad couldn't afford him—and put him back on an hourly rate.

Early on, he mowed yards in Pittsburg, picked peaches, hauled hay, sacked groceries at Piggly Wiggly, and, later, worked summers at Lone Star Steel.

I met Mike at East Texas State University in 1979 (now Texas A&M University-Commerce) while we were members of Sigma Chi Fraternity. Mike's brother, Joe, was a member and several of his friends from East Texas had pledged. The Fraternity had recently built a huge lodge, eight A-frame cabins for brothers to live in, a swimming pool and other amenities. Quite a hefty financial burden for a group of Fraternity guys!

We were having trouble paying the bills and Mike Cavender—or Clyde as he was called—had a brainstorm. Somehow he got hold of a projector and a copy of a movie *everyone* wanted to see. Now, this was way before VCRs and movie rentals and most of these East Texas boys had never seen a movie like this!

Anyway, Mike sold tickets for $5. The Sigma Chi lodge was so crowded that we had to rewind and show the movie over. Because of the demand, we had the same event the next week. Remarkably, the Fraternity had a financial boost, and we were back in business!

Mike graduated from East Texas State University in 1982 and began working in the family business in May. Since then, his life has been a whirlwind. Not only is he in charge of company operations, with the recent opening of the 41st store in Texas, but he also oversees finance, human resources, real estate and construction, and helps keep track of the largest boot inventory in the world.

He is known for his calm demeanor and thoughtful approach to serving the needs of the customer and his employees. His mama raised him to consider others and that's evident in his many philanthropic projects with the American Cancer Society, Justin Boot's Cowboy Crisis Fund, and the Texas A&M University-Commerce Foundation Board.

As we say in Texas, he's a good egg!

Sincerely,

Larry Goddard

Larry Goddard
Associate Vice President-Development

Development Office
P.O. Box 3425, Commerce, Texas 75429-3425   (903) 886-5513   Fax: (903) 886-5711

I asked Larry Goddard to write my "Tall Texas Tale" because: *Of our long friendship, which goes way back to 1979 when I first met Larry. He was a straight A student at East Texas State University (now Texas A&M University—Commerce). Needless to say, I was not in his class with the brains, but we became Sigma Chi fraternity brothers and remain very good friends to this day.*

"His mama raised him to consider others . . ."

"Rome wasn't built in a day,

SELLS MORE COWBOY BOOTS THAN ANYONE IN THE WORLD!

My Texas post is: Cavender's Boot City. You'll find me in a Cavender's Boot City store near you.

I was born & raised in: Pittsburg, TX—my parents still live there.

I hang my hat in: Bullard, TX, about 12 miles south of Tyler.

I came into this world: On the night of October 20, 1957, as Mickey Mantle celebrated his 26th birthday.

I'm a real cowboy because: We're going to "make it" next year (in the ranching operation).

If you run into any of my friends ask them: How many times a day I brush my teeth! And how many places I have a toothbrush stashed . . . just in case.

If you walked a mile in my boots: You'd say, "These are great boots, I'll have to ask him where he gets 'em."

My ultimate Texas date would be: Simply a nice dinner at one of the many great Texas restaurants.

I love Texas because: Texans are the most hospitable of all.

but we weren't running that job."

— Mike's Favorite Texas Saying

JOSÉ CISNEROS
ILLUSTRATOR OF THE TEXAS VAQUERO

DECLARED "A LIVING LEGEND" BY THE WESTERNERS INTERNATIONAL & RECEIVED NATIONAL COWBOY HALL OF FAME WRANGLER AWARD

My Texas post is: My home in El Paso, TX, surrounded by the Franklin Mountains.

I came into this world on: April 18, 1910 in the middle of the Mexican Revolution!

I was born and raised in: Born in the small town of Durango, Mexico and came to El Paso, TX at age 15 in 1925.

I hang my hat in: I don't wear a hat—just the hair on my head.

I'm a real cowboy because: Though I've never ridden a horse it has been the main subject of my life's work . . . the vaquero!

If you run into my friend Dr. John West ask him: About the book he wrote about me called *An Artist's Journey.* He knows all about me and likes to kid about my age. I'm 90 now. He thinks I've lived too long.

If you walked a mile in my boots: You would have had the privilege of putting your boots under Sam Houston's bed in the Texas Governor's Mansion.

I love Texas because: It is my second home. I've lived here longer than anywhere, since 1925. I am a Texas native.

"I'll die with a pen in my hand."

— Jose's Favorite Texas Saying

" . . . 'I made a commitment to follow their hoof prints along and across the land.'"

I asked Laura Bush to write my "Tall Texas Tale"
because: *She is a good friend. She had a reception for me and my work at the Governor's Mansion. You can't find a better friend than that.*

OFFICE OF LAURA W. BUSH

April 6, 2000

Dear Martana:

To me, Jose Cisneros is a living symbol of the wondrously diverse cultures, imaginations and success stories that color our state's rich heritage. We seem too often these days to hear about what is wrong or broken or failing in our society. It is, of course, admirable always to strive for improvement.

But the inspiration for that improvement, the hope that almost anything is possible in our society if you just dream wildly enough and work hard enough, springs from seeing and celebrating the achievements of people like Jose Cisneros.

In some societies you are what you were born. In ours, you are born to become whatever you want. Jose was born into a revolution he knew nothing about. He became in Texas a renowned artist in a field where he had no formal training. He taught himself to read. He taught himself to research history. He taught himself to draw. He taught himself to "see" the many beauties in colors, despite being colorblind. And through these personal achievements—and his own powerful modesty--Jose Cisneros has taught all of us to "see" our own history through his works of art. His drawings are truly invitations to learn about ourselves and our heritages.

As John O. West has written, "His story rivals the novels of Horatio Alger, but the story of Jose Cisneros is a true one."

After once drawing a band of historical horses, Jose said, "I made a commitment to follow their hoof prints along and across the land."

Fortunately, through his insights and skills, Jose has allowed millions of people over the decades—including my husband and me--to make that journey along with him. We are both deeply appreciative.

Sincerely,

Laura Bush

POST OFFICE BOX 1902, AUSTIN, TEXAS 78767 PHONE 512/637-2000 FAX 512/637-8800 WWW.GEORGEWBUSH.COM
NOT PRINTED OR MAILED AT TAXPAYER EXPENSE.
PAID FOR BY BUSH FOR PRESIDENT, INC.

JACK CODY
ENGLISH TEACHER & THEATRE DIRECTOR

TEXAS TEACHER OF THE YEAR 2000!

My Texas post is: English Department Chairperson and Theatre Director, Graham High School, Graham, TX and in the classroom with students.

I came into this world on: A breezy June day and my life has been an endless summer.

I was born & raised in: Winfield and Mount Pleasant in Titus County, TX.

I hang my hat in: The lobby of any good theatre to enter the dream world created by the world's most fascinating writers populated by the world's most fascinating people—actors! After that, my hat is at home on Elm Street with friends sharing experiences and making our own theatre happenings. Eventually, my hat makes its way to Sante Fe so I can refresh my soul.

I'm a real cowboy because: I married a real cowgirl, Diane, who rode horses before she walked, worked cattle before she went to school, taught western riding to greenhorns and married me to certify my cowboy image!

If you run into my friends ask them about: The "poverty" vacations to Garner State Park; summer conventions; New Year's Eve parties; breaking out or into school parties; trips to NYC; or just their favorite memory of the Codys!

If you walked a mile in my boots: You would understand the challenges, the rewards, and the thrills of knowing today's youth—there's security in knowing who will be taking care of you in your twilight years.

I love Texas because: It offers me everything from forests to prairies, from swamps to deserts, from oceans to mountains—inhabited with gifted people from many cultures willing to lock arms and march into the next century together!

"Watch what you say; when you put your foot in your mouth, leather is hard to chew."

— Jack's Favorite Texas Saying

Charles Shafer

Dear Martana,

Jack Cody, even as a kid in the 1940's and 50's, showed traces of the distinction he would later achieve. Jack was my best friend for a multitude of reasons. His name alone sounded like that of a character from the Zane Grey westerns I devoured with great zest; in fact, Jack insisted that he was a direct descendant of Buffalo Bill Cody. Of course, the fact that he had a small gray mare which he rode to town occasionally only substantiated my belief that there were indeed some bonafide western remnants in the lanky kid from Winfield, Texas.

Jack endeared himself to me even more when he encouraged me to ride his little gray mare. What he failed to tell me was that the mare knew only one direction and speed -- straight ahead at a full gallop. Bent double with laughter, he watched as the mare raced across the schoolyard and I tried desperately to stay in the saddle (a task I never accomplished for more than a hundred yards). Even though the mare was no Trigger, Champ, or Silver, at least she remotely resembled the steeds we'd seen in countless Randolph Scott westerns at the Texan Theater in Mount Pleasant. It was probably Jack's mare that discouraged my becoming a fulltime cowboy as planned.

Jack Cody was also a contradiction. In addition to his equestrian skills, he played the piano. Most kids in Winfield figured that any fourth-grade boy who was an accomplished pianist probably also ate spinach while smiling obediently and listening to public radio rather than the usual fare (*The Green Hornet, Inner Sanctum, The Six Shooter, Fibber McGee and Molly*) like the rest of us. However, no one ever questioned his manhood after he rescued his fellow fourth-grade boys from the bully who had delighted in terrorizing us at recess through most of the year, and he did it with as much confidence and grace as I'd ever seen a bully dispatched.

The high-school years came and went, and Jack and I went to East Texas State College (now Texas A&M University at Commerce) where as roommates we endured together the insufferable homesickness of country kids who had spent very few days or nights away from home. When we graduated in 1963, we went in different directions to make our marks on our worlds. After thirty-seven years, I was delighted but not surprised to learn that my old friend had been named Texas' Secondary Teacher of the Year. You see, Jack had always had a noble calling, even as a little boy from small-town Texas who let me ride his horse and who drove evil from our midst.

Sincerely,

Charles Shafer

Charles Shafer

"**. . . Jack insisted that he was a direct descendant of Buffalo Bill Cody.**"

I asked Charles Shafer to write my "Tall Texas Tale" because: *He is a creative writer and can make me sound good.*

ROY COOPER
"SUPER LOOPER," ALL-AMERICAN ROPER

8-TIME WORLD CHAMPION COWBOY & PRO-RODEO ALL-TIME LEADING MONEY WINNER

My Texas post is: Rodeo arenas across the country. My favorite places to rodeo are the Houston Astrodome, Fort Worth and San Antonio.

I came into this world on: November 13, 1955—ridin' and ropin'.

I hang my hat in: Childress, TX— on the edge of the Panhandle on the high plains of Texas.

I'm a real cowboy because: was born to be.

If you run into my friend Tommy Guy ask him about the time I: Was test driving a motor home. I wrecked it.

If you walked a mile in my boots: You would have traveled a lot of miles and roped in a lot of rodeos.

I love Texas because: Texas is where it's at!

"You can always tell a Texan, but you can't tell him much!"

— Roy's Favorite Texas Saying

Smith Brothers

Dear Martana,

If Steven Spielberg followed Roy Cooper around with a movie camera, Roy would have provided a story that would have'em lining up around the block to watch. With Roy Cooper, 8-time World Champion Rodeo Cowboy, life's always going in fifty different directions...if Spielberg could only catch up with him! Let me elaborate a bit here with a few humorous examples that best represent life with Roy Cooper.

Roy's longtime friend, Oklahoma oilman Marshall Brackin was pulling Roy's horse "Big Time John" from a rodeo in Florida on the way to Dallas. He got as far as New Orleans, when he found out that Mardi Gras was in full swing! Never one to miss a good party, Marshall decided he wanted to stay and have a little fun. Problem was, he had Roy's horse with him. So he decided that if he just rented a hotel room for the night, he could leave the horse in style while he hit Bourbon Street.

Back in those days, the New Orleans Howard Johnsons didn't really allow horses of famed rodeo stars in their hotels. So Marshall snuck the horse through the back door and up the service elevator to his 9th floor hotel room. He filled the tub full of water, gave "Big Time John" a bale of hay and left the horse in the room—while he went out and engaged in the Mardi Gras festivities. As the sun was coming up the next morning, Marshall was coming in— only to find the local sheriff waiting for him in the hotel room. Apparently, the maid had come in to do some housekeeping and nearly had a heart attack when she saw Roy's horse. The sheriff gave Marshall a stern warning as Marshall walked the horse down the hall, to the main elevator, through the lobby (where Sunday brunch was in full swing) and back to the trailer. Needless to say, the sheriff gave Marshall and "Big Time John" a personal escort out of town. When they reached the Louisiana border, the sheriff said, "Go ahead, big ticket. You are excused from town and you are not exactly welcome back." Roy's horse never got to stay in a Howard Johnsons again!

On another occasion, a big group of us were up at Ed Gaylord's "Lazy E Ranch" in Guthrie, Oklahoma where the National Steer Ropin' Finals are held. (It's the timed event championship of the world where twenty of the best cowboys in the country—Roy being one—compete in calf roping, steer wrestling, steer roping, and heading & heeling.)

When the event was over, Roy invited fifteen family and friends to the Outback Steakhouse in Oklahoma City. It was at this point in the night that Roy starts talking about a horse that he had ridden that day in the competition. He said, "You know, I think we should all chip in $2,500 each and buy that horse." Vincent Russell, owner of the Oklahoma City Goodyear Tire Co., decided that he would go to the trailer and lead the horse into the Outback Steakhouse so that everyone could get a good look at the horse before we made our decision to buy. As Vince was walkin' the horse in, a guy walking out started talkin' like an auctioneer saying "were starting out at $250 dollars...$250...$250...anyone want to bid $300 here?" Roy calls out, "fifteen thousand!" and Vince yells "SOLD! To the cowboy at the Outback!"

Roy did for the rodeo world what Michael Jordan did for basketball. Roy's a true Rodeo Champion whose greatness as a Cowboy has taken roping to a whole new level. He is a character right out of a movie, a loyal friend, a man indebted to his wonderful wife and children, a hero, a great horseman and a guy born to stardom. Mr. Spielberg, are you ever missing out!

Jim Smith

PS. The horse we bought that night was named SNIPER—he's one of the greatest ropin' horses ever purchased in a restaurant!

" The Premier Catalog for the Western Horseman"

Smith Brothers

Address
7833 &I-35

Denton,
America(TX)
76207-1531

Phone
940-387-6772

Fax
940-565-8232

Website
www.smithbros.com

"Back in those days, the New Orleans Howard Johnsons didn't really allow horses of famed rodeo stars in their hotels."

I asked Jim Smith to write my "Tall Texas Tale" because: *He's been my sidekick from the start; A Cowboy Gentleman from the heart; A true and loyal friend through it all—that's what makes him Texas Tall!!*

MARK CUBAN
INTERNET TRAILBLAZER

MADE MORE THAN 200 BROADCAST.COM EMPLOYEES MILLIONAIRES!

My Texas Post is: Co-founder of broadcast.com and owner of the Dallas Mavericks.

I hang my hat in: The new silicon valley . . . Dallas, TX.

I came into this world: On July 31.com.

I'm a real cowboy because: I like Shiner beer.

If you run into my friend Michael ask him about: My very short-lived acting career. He would say if there was an Oscar for fast-food auditions, I'd have a mantel full.

If you walked a mile in my boots (loafers): You would have been a billionaire for 48 hours!

My ultimate Texas date would be: A Mavs basketball game & a steak dinner at Del Friscos.

I love Texas because: It's fun! The energy here is incredible.

"Work hard, play harder."

— Mark's Favorite Texas Saying

MARK STAHL

"Cuban runs on Wall Street rather than the hardwood."

I asked Mark Stahl to write my "Tall Texas Tale"

because: *He's been my running buddy for a long time. He's seen me tell a "Texas tale" or two, and he's played a part in more than a few of those tales.*

Dear Martana,

In the fall of 1995, pickup basketball dominated Mark Cuban's routine. By 4 p.m. every afternoon, he had his hoop shoes laced and his name up on the players' board at Dallas' Premier Club. The biggest concerns of his day were making the "First 10" and "dominating" the court so his team could keep the "run" the entire afternoon.

Then he stopped coming to the court. The close-knit group of hoopers noticed Cuban's absence, but no one knew what he was up to until one day a two-page article appeared in the Dallas Morning News about a new company called Audionet. Utilizing a new technology, the two-man startup had begun broadcasting the taped-delayed signal of Dallas radio station KLIF over the World Wide Web. In the photo accompanying the story, there was Mark, their fellow hoopster, standing in a computer room with a group of radio executives and business partner Todd Wagner. Of course, Mark was the only one in jeans and a T-shirt.

It wasn't long before the infant technology that Audionet utilized advanced to the point where Audionet could broadcast the live feed from KLIF. Using the Web, Audionet was capable of sending KLIF's signal to every corner of the world. That is when, sitting in front of his personal computer in a small home office, Cuban knew with certainty that he had the future of media at his fingertips. At first, the company concentrated on acquiring sports content, specifically, college sports. College alumni could tune into the action of their alma maters' teams no matter where they lived.

Wagner and Cuban started building Audionet one college at a time. They hired salespeople and network gurus. At the same time they were acquiring the Internet broadcasting rights to college sports, they were also convincing other radio stations to follow KLIF's lead into cyberspace. One station at a time, they built Audionet's lineup of broadcasters.

Eventually, Audionet outgrew its first office and moved to a nearby building ten times the size of the original. Technology advanced so quickly that within two years, not just audio but video became viable on the Net with Audionet leading the way. To better address the new market, Audionet changed its name to Broadcast.com and planned an initial public offering. You've probably read about it.

Working through the ups and downs of the market and the company's recent acquisition by Internet giant Yahoo has required more long days and nights. Broadcast.com employees will tell you the dude never sleeps. At the same time, the "dude's vision has brought them more excitement, new-media business experience and wealth than they could otherwise have imagined.

And although Cuban's name is no longer on the player board at the Premier Club, the company's name appears on a much bigger board - the NASDAQ. His daily concerns still revolve around his "run," "dominating" and making the "First Ten." Cuban runs on Wall Street rather than the hardwood. He "dominates" an industry, Internet broadcasting. Going to the "net" has taken on a whole new meaning and the "First Ten" is now a conceivable goal for Fortune magazine's list of world wealthiest people.

Sincerely,

Mark Stahl

Mark Stahl

EDDIE DEEN
BEST BBQ & CATERER IN TEXAS

I asked Ray Hunt to write my "Tall Texas Tale" because: *I like him, I trust him and he helped me realize the potential that I had in the catering business. He is a truly good example of how my business evolved by just giving an ol' boy from East Texas a chance to prove himself.*

"Who knows what inaugural event he might serve next?"

RAY L. HUNT
FOUNTAIN PLACE
1445 ROSS AT FIELD
DALLAS, TEXAS 75202-2785

November 29, 1999

Dear Martana,

I know a man who wears a white cowboy hat and does business in the small town of Terrell, just east of Dallas. He can bring a pleasant smile to the face of every Texan who likes, or maybe I should say appreciates, great Texas barbecue. His name is Eddie Deen and his fame has spread as fast or even faster than the waistlines of his friends and hungry customers.

Eddie started his small business just to serve the local folks in town. But nearby ranches, such as the Circle K, were in need of catered services for various events and Eddie's food came highly recommended. He knew his business and everything about the food he prepared: the proper aging of the meats; the cuts and textures; the right temperature for cooking that would leave them tender and moist; and the best smoking techniques to impart a flavor to savor and remember. He could tell you or your guests about it in fascinating detail.

Before too long his reputation spread, one could truthfully say, by word of mouth, to Dallas. The aromas of his catered corporate lunches began to fill elevator lobbies and high rise halls with indescribably delicious smells and his brand of Texas cuisine was sought after throughout the city and beyond.

His reputation had grown, but was he able to handle, say, fifteen thousand people in an hour? Governor Bush thought so, and that's why Eddie Deen's barbecue catered the first Bush inaugural luncheon on the grounds of the capitol in Austin. Then, as if to prove the point, he did it again at the second Bush inaugural. Who knows what inaugural event he might serve next?

Although Eddie's fame has spread throughout the state, his roots remain in Terrell. Oh, one last thing. I suppose we shouldn't mention all the special things he does for schools, churches and charities to make life easier for those who need a hand. Someone might get the idea he's a nice guy.

Let's just say I am proud to know Eddie Deen, a friend and fellow Texan.

Sincerely,

Ray L. Hunt

Fed 15,500 People in 38 Minutes at Governor Bush's '99 Inaugural!

My Texas post is: Eddie Deen & Co. catering & Eddie Deen's Ranch, downtown Dallas.

I hang my hat in: Wills Point, TX, with the people I love in the place that I call home.

I was born & raised in: Wills Point, TX, where the cotton field met the football field.

I came into this world on: September 5, 1956, on the shoulders of a good family that taught me to be tough when I had to be and showed me a hard working day, but it took a good woman to show me the softer and gentler ways.

I'm a real cowboy because: I own a ranch in downtown Dallas and I was born and raised on a horse.

If you run into one of the guests ask them about: My piano playing. They will tell you they saw me play at the Cattle Baron's Ball or the Texas Men event, "A Lone Star Night." (No one has suggested I give up my day job yet!)

If you walked a mile in my boots: You would smell like hickory smoke.

My ultimate Texas date would be: Any event that I am not the caterer!

I love Texas because: We've got the best BBQ, the best football and it's no coincidence that Miss Texas makes the national finals every year!

"Well it's just a couple of Aggies building a bonfire on the Capital lawn & the only thing missing was Bevo."

— Eddie's Favorite Texas Saying

DAVID DIKE
LONE STAR ART IMPRESARIO

SHOWCASING TEXAS HERITAGE BY EXHIBITING & REDISCOVERING TEXAS ARTISTS (1880-1950)

My Texas post is: David Dike Fine Art of Texas. We appeal to cowboys, ranchers and just about everyone else y'all!

I came into this world on: October 17, 1959 on a colorful day.

I was born & raised in: Cowtown, better known as Fort Worth, TX—where the West begins.

I hang my hat in: The Hall. (Not the Dance Hall!)

I'm a real cowboy because: I appreciate Texas art, I sell Texas art, I eat, sleep and drink Texas art.

If you run into my friend Bob from Amarillo ask him about the time: He shot me on accident while we were dove hunting. Lucky for me that day he wasn't a very good shot, but too bad for him, since he didn't catch any dove!

If you walked a mile in my boots: You better like Bluebonnets.

I love Texas because: Where else could they have filmed *Giant*?

"Big hat, no cattle."

— David's Favorite Texas Saying

"I left my husband in intensive care to attend David's auction."

DIAN MALOUF

David Dike pioneered Texas Regionalism when few of us were aware it existed. He has educated us so well and made collecting so exciting, I left my husband in intensive care to attend David's auction—

Dian Malouf

P.S. my husband Andy lived (he still loves me too) he didn't kill me

PPS. The Art I bought that night looks great!

I asked Dian Malouf to write my "Tall Texas Tale" because: *As the author of* Cattle Kings of Texas, *Dian shares my dream of preserving the heritage of Texas. She's been a long-time patron and supporter of my gallery, David Dike Fine Art of Texas.*

CLAY DUNCAN
WIRELESS INTERNET PATHFINDER

I asked Peter Boyd to write my "Tall Texas Tale" because: *He not only shares a devoted appreciation for Texas' legends and lore, but also is a personal family friend with a great wit and sense of humor.*

" . . . as well as having a great, great uncle who was Texas Governor Thomas Mitchell Campbell (1907-1911)."

SOUTHSIDEBANK

P.O. BOX 1079, SOUTH BECKHAM AT EAST LAKE, TYLER, TEXAS 75710-1079   903/531-7111   Fax: 903/592-3692

PETER M. BOYD
EXECUTIVE VICE PRESIDENT

October 7, 1999

Ms. Martana Hanson, Publisher
Texas Men
25 Highland Park Village, Suite 100-140
Dallas, Texas 75205

Dear Martana:

As you know, Texas is a wonderful State owning an exciting past, a dazzling present and a radiant future. While these three outstanding traits rarely appear together, they are all mirrored in seventh-generation Texan, Clay Duncan. The final image in that mirror represents the very best of Texas and of its Texas men.

Clay comes from a long line of proud, distinguished Texans. On one side of his family his provenance includes a great, great, great grandfather who served as a Captain under General Hood in the War between the States, as well as having a great, great uncle who was Texas Governor Thomas Mitchell Campbell (1907-1911). From his father's family comes lineage to John Duncan Young, a noted Texas Ranger and founder of Fort Duncan in Richland Springs, outside of San Saba. This side of Clay's family was of hearty stock and includes cattlemen-trail bosses and drovers, Indian fighters, pioneers, scouts and gamblers. All are part of our diverse heritage and all are incorporated into the melting pot that is our Texas of today.

Which brings us to the present. After receiving his graduate business degree from Southern Methodist and working on the West Coast with a California investment management firm, Clay, like his Texas ancestors, went out and blazed his own trail while looking into the Millennium-a trail of advanced technology with an entrepreneurial vision. After focusing on global telecommunications by forming and managing several international concerns, Clay has recently returned to his native Texas, being associated with a start-up wireless broadband provider in the Metroplex. Truly he personifies the adventurous spirit of the Duncan family while using his keen intuition, winning smile, calm disposition and the fortitude to take that calculated risk. Surely the future is glowing for Clay and us all, as through his endeavors, international barriers are being erased with the world becoming more and more Texan!

Long Live That Texas Spirit,

Peter M. Boyd
Executive Vice President

Member
FDIC

SEVENTH-GENERATION TEXAN

My Texas post is: In Dallas, connecting Texas to the world through Clearwire wireless Internet access.

I hang my hat in: My Deep Ellum loft where I enjoy the serenity of sunrises and the warmth of pleasant surroundings.

I was born & raised in: Born in Dallas & raised in Tyler, TX, the Rose Capital of Texas.

I came into this world on: October 21, 1968, all smiles.

I'm a real cowboy because: No matter where I am in the world, people immediately assume I'm a Texan.

If you run into my friends ask them about my: Concho belt that brands me as a true Texan. The conchos were designed to commemorate the 150-year anniversary of Texas' independence. Since it is a gift that belonged to my larger-than-life Grandfather, it represents sentimental and fond memories for me.

If you walked a mile in my boots: You would have surfed 15-foot swells off the coast of Costa Rica.

My ultimate Texas date would be: A Harley ride to the Hill Country for a sunset picnic at Fort Duncan, founded by my ancestors in the 1840s.

I love Texas because: Of that fiercely independent and "can-do" Texas state-of-mind.

"Seek not your resting place in the earth, but in the hearts of men."

— Clay's Favorite Texas Saying

H. MILLS DUNCAN IV
TEXAS' FINEST COFFEE ROASTER

August C. Bering, IV
Chairman & C.E.O.

Dear Martana,

I will never forget the first time H. Mills Duncan, IV walked into my office and gave me a sales pitch on buying his coffee beans. Here was a thin, tall, lanky likeable fellow who wanted to waste about 20 minutes of my time.

I had met Mills several years earlier and knew him to be involved in the commercial real estate business, but did not know him to know beans about coffee beans. Bering's prides itself in providing only the finest goods to our customers. After a careful nationwide search we selected a coffee vendor located in Oregon. Their product was good and we had no complaints. I asked why we should give him the opportunity to sell us coffee when at the time he was brand new in the business and still working in the real estate industry to support his coffee venture.

After about an hour visit he had convinced me that he could supply our needs with fresher coffee and better service. I then asked him, "What's your price?" He replied, "Don't you worry about the price, I'll be cheaper and better than anyone else." It was classic BS. I found out later that at the time, Mills had forgotten his price sheet and couldn't remember how much he would charge! After a short meeting with our buyers we decided to give the "home town boy" a try.

Mills has exceeded our expectations, has always made good on his promises, and not only is he one of our top vendors, but also a great friend. I have gotten to know Mills as a man of integrity, a family man, and a good citizen. I wish him great success in his quest to again make the Duncan name synonymous with quality coffee in our community.

Sincerely,

A. C. Bering IV

August C. Bering, IV

6102 Westheimer   Houston, Texas 77057   (713) 785-6400
3900 Bissonnet at Weslayan   Houston, Texas 77005   (713) 665-0500

I asked Augie Bering to write my "Tall Texas Tale" because: *In true Texas style, Augie gave me my start in the coffee business by allowing me to take over his gourmet coffee business at his world famous Bering Hardware store.*

" . . . 'Don't you worry about the price, I'll be cheaper and better than anyone else.' It was classic BS."

Brought Back the Century-Old Family Duncan Coffee Business

My Texas post is: Duncan Coffee Company World Headquarters, Houston, TX.

I came into this world on: February 8, 1964—looking for a double shot of espresso.

I was born & raised in: Born in Houston, TX and raised in bars, beer joints and coffee shops around the world.

I hang my hat in: Houston, TX, 8.5 miles from the rich folk.

I'm a real cowboy because: I don't wear my hat only once a year at the Houston Livestock Show.

If you run into my friend Larry Padget ask him about the time: The two cowboys tried to take my hat. He'll tell ya I still got it. And their teeth for souvenirs.

If you walked a mile in my boots: You'd have too many kids, too much responsibility and the Lord would have blessed you way too much.

I love Texas because: Where else can a girl named Martana publish a book like this?

"There is a hell of a lot of business out there. I just want more than my fair share!"

— Mills' Favorite Texas Saying

GARY DUNSHEE
SADDLEMAKER OF THE WEST
MAKING SADDLES FOR COWPUNCHERS THAT SPEND THEIR LIVES ON HORSEBACK

My Texas post is: President of Big Bend Saddlery, Alpine, TX— where we outfit cowboys throughout the West.

I came into this world on: August 11, 1950.

I hang my hat in: Brewster County, TX, at the foot of Mount Ord.

I'm a real cowboy because: Good try, but no cigar. However, I am fortunate to be able to work with cowboys and their families on a daily basis.

If you run into my friends, Rex Ivey, Fred Dalby or Lynn Coffey, ask them about the time we: Chased a steer from the Washington Monument to the Kennedy Center on horseback. We told them the arena was too small for roping. And sure enough, that steer got through the Bicentennial celebration, clear across town! It took us 15 minutes to get our horses through the crowd and cold-trail him to an underground parking lot at the Kennedy Center.

If you walked a mile in my boots: You would meet some mighty fine folks and families who make their living on horseback— whose only care is to be left unchanged by a fast-changing world.

I love Texas because: Of the friendly folks, their traditional values—God, family and friends—and their deep-rooted respect for our state's heritage.

"Any man that can make a living doing what he likes is lucky . . . and I'm that. Any time I cash in now, I win!"

— Gary's Favorite Texas Saying

"When we got inside, something just wasn't right. There were no women!"

I asked Bret Collier to write my "Tall Texas Tale" because: *I paid him $20 and told him not to write anything stupid.*

Big Bend Saddlery, Inc.

Box 58 Alpine Tx 79831
(915) 837-5551

Dear Martana:

With over thirty years of experience, Gary Dunshee has handcrafted 100's of saddles for working cowboys all over the world! Many celebrities, such as Charlie Daniels and Tom Sellek, have also bought Big Bend saddles.

Besides his great skill as a saddle maker, Gary is also a genuinely good guy. He has employed more than 20 students from Sul Ross State University and provided jobs for students (including myself) so that they could go to college and work at the same time. Gary is an inspiration to all of us because of his dedication to the craft of saddle making, his patience, faith, even temper, and fairness.

He also has a pretty good sense of humor about life's mishaps. For example, one day back in the early 80's, Gary and I flew to Dallas to buy some things at the Apparel Mart. We were well dressed for the trip to the big city--wearing our suit coats with starched Wranglers, boots, and cowboy hats.

After we had done our work at the Mart, we stopped outside and asked a cab driver where we could go get a drink. He said, "Hop in. I know a place for you two." He drove us around and dropped us off saying, "I think you'll find a good place around here."
Well, I gave him a big tip because he had been so cordial to us and Gary and I hopped out of the cab. The driver had dropped us off in front of a place called "JR's Bigger Than Dallas." Gary said he thought he had maybe seen an ad for the place in Texas Monthly, so we decided to try the place out for a drink or two.

When we got inside, something just wasn't right. There were no women! I mean to say that every table was a man with a man. Gary and I looked at each other, and bolted for the door! Outside, we saw that ALL the bars in that area were "like that" and I told Gary, "Let's get outa here." As we were trying to flag down another cab, a group of Sunday drivers drove by. They had their windows down, and I heard a woman say, "Look honey! Two cowboy ones!"

Needless to say, when Gary and I fly to Dallas and take a cab, we are VERY specific about what kind of place we want, and even more specific about what kind we don't want!

Gary is a quality person with both a great work ethic and an equally good sense of humor. He produces saddles of only the finest material, and he won't give his final approval until everything is right. He's the kind of guy you naturally trust.

Bret Collier
Vice-President
Big Bend Saddlery

Any man that can make a living doing what he like's is lucky.

MARK EDDINS
AUTO INDUSTRY ENTREPRENEUR

KNOWN AROUND THE INDUSTRY AS ALWAYS BEING ON THE BLOODY EDGE

My Texas post is: President, Friendly Chevrolet in Dallas, TX.

I came into this world on: October 30, 1950 on two wheels.

I hang my hat in: Dallas, TX.

I'm a real cowboy because: . . . Well, I'm really not a cowboy.

If you run into my friend Chris ask him about the time I: Dressed up like the "Joker" for Halloween. I studied the look, actions and personality style of the Joker character and my costume was complete with prosthetics, the hair, lime green tux, purple pants, yellow shirt, etc. I had all the gestures and mannerisms down pat! It was a hoot, and no one recognized me [as Mark] either.

If you walked a mile in my boots: You'd probably get blisters!

My ultimate Texas date would be: A date with Heather Locklear.

I love Texas because: It usually has great seasons, the people are great and Texas has a tremendous diversity of scenery from all four corners.

"Everything's bigger in Texas."

— Mark's Favorite Texas Saying

BYRNE COMPANY

Wednesday, November 17, 1999

Dear Martana,

TAKING CHARGE, TAKING RISKS, AND TAKING NO PRISONERS. No words could better define Mark Eddins.

1983 was the year I met Mark Eddins. Life was good, real estate was booming. Automobile sales were great, and Friendly Chevrolet was one of the top Chevy dealers in the state. Mark Eddins was on a roll. I thought I was "hyper" until I met Mark. In our first meeting, several facts became very evident: "you better know your business," "you better shoot straight," "you better be able to sell yourself," and "you better be able to act fast." Anything short of that and you'd be left behind.

Mark started working in the automobile business in junior high school, and worked his way to the top at Friendly Chevrolet. Mark Eddins knew what he wanted, and he knew how to get it.

Fast forward: early 1990's. Life ain't so great. Texas had just suffered the worst recession (I hope I never see a depression) in modern times. Friendly Chevrolet's sales were 70% **less** than they were in the mid-1980's. Their facilities were dated, their lease was expiring, their parts department had just burned down, they had too much real estate, too much debt, and they were losing money fast. (I'm not sure how you lose money slow.) Most of us would have folded our tent out of despair and gone to the house.

Mark called me. He was ready to do battle. During Friendly Chevrolet's darkest hours, he had a vision. After 40 years in the same location, Mark wanted to relocate Friendly Chevrolet and build a new world-class automobile facility. Mark wanted to sell all his facilities and consolidate into one location, but in order to do this, he had to overcome three years of hurdles and take on even more debt. "Was he crazy?" His sales would not justify the cost. "He's gonna go broke," and "He's paying too much money for the land," said the naysayers.

1999. Life is grand. Mark Eddins has relocated Friendly Chevrolet. Business is great. Friendly Chevrolet's sales are booming.

Mark and I had lunch a few weeks ago. I believe he'd do it all over again … just for the fun of it.

Mark Eddins embodies the true Texas spirit: "Never, never, ever give up."

Regards,

Sean M. Byrne

8525 Ferndale Road   Suite 100   Dallas, Texas 75238-4423   214-343-6996   Fax: 214-343-6998

"I believe he'd do it all over again . . . just for the fun of it."

I asked Sean Byrne to write my "Tall Texas Tale" because: *He's a long-time trusted friend. He has great perspective and is probably the most completely "in control" guy I've met.*

ARLO EISENBERG
ROLLERBLADING OUTLAW

NATIONAL IN-LINE SKATE SERIES CHAMPION
& X GAMES CHAMPION

My Texas post is: Eisenbergs Skate Park in Plano, TX and co-founder of Senate—wheel and accessory firm.

I came into this world on: Eight wheels, September 7, 1973.

I was born and raised in: Born in St. Paul Medical Hospital in Dallas, TX and raised at Skatetime at Bachman Lake.

I hang my hat in: Long Beach, CA, but I hang my helmet in Plano, TX.

I'm a real cowboy because: I make my living wearing boots.

If you run into my friend Steve Ratliff ask him about my: Senior picture at Arts Magnet. Actually, don't ask him about it. In fact, never mention it again . . . to anyone.

If you walked a mile in my boots: You'd be missing the point.

My ultimate Texas date would be: At the Inwood, because then no matter how things turned out, at the very least I would have seen a good movie.

I love Texas because: It provided me with a unique perspective. Dallas was a big enough city that I was always aware of the rest of the world, but small enough that I was never too jaded by it.

"It's not how hard you fall, it's how good it looks on video."

— Arlo's Favorite Texas Saying

November 12, 1999

Dear Martana,

Fifteen years ago, Arlo Eisenberg hung around backstage at the first annual World Drive-In Movie Festival and Custom Car Rally, where I got to know him as an intense but amiable 10-year-old who seemed to listen to signals from another planet. (I mean this in a good way.) Then, five years ago, Arlo became the first world champion in in-line street skating when he won the Taco Bell National In-Line Skate Series in Venice, California, out-pointing twenty other skaters from around the world. His aggressive style was impressive enough, but I was even more impressed with his ability to corner every endorsement possible, including deals with competing sponsors!

Arlo is considered the number one celebrity in the world in a sport that is half about athleticism and half about pure chutzpah. He considers himself a skating ambassador, travelling more or less constantly to competitions all over the globe and giving demonstrations, while at the same time running his own company, Senate, which is, of course, the outlaw among wheel-and-accessory firms. (He sells, among other things, those baggy pants that are de rigeur among skaters.) He has performed in the closing ceremonies of the 1994 Olympics; edited Daily Bread magazine, the first publication dedicated to aggressive in-line skating; won the X Games; hosted his own show on Fox Sports; and starred in some of the most radical skate videos ever made. Arlo is, in a world of cool, a block of solid ice.

Arlo is, to put it mildly, banged up. All aggressive street skaters are banged up, but Arlo belongs in the hall of skating's lionhearts. His greatest moment, I think, is one that you may have already seen, because MTV loves to show it again and again. Arlo hops onto a four-foot-high iron railing and slides down it at such a steep angle that he has to hold his arms like a floundering eagle and try to avoid the moment most feared by in-line skaters everywhere. But the moment comes. He drops directly onto his crotch, and the life goes out of his body. He falls to his left and writhes around on the ground, face contorted in a horrible grimace, as skate groupies converge. Perhaps you will, and perhaps you won't, be able to realize why such a moment is what defines a street skating king. Arlo's first words, once he regains the power of speech: "Did you get it?"

He was speaking, of course, to the cameraman. He didn't hang around at my film festivals without learning a thing or two about getting the money shot.

Sincerely,

Joe Bob Briggs

JOE BOB BRIGGS
P.O. BOX 2002
DALLAS, TX 75221

"Arlo is, in a world of cool, a block of solid ice."

I asked Joe Bob Briggs to write my "Tall Texas Tale" because: *I admire his independent spirit and because his background reviewing drive-in movies, that most people find offensive, makes him uniquely qualified to editorialize about my unconventional career.*

JIM FISHER
REAL ESTATE DREAM MAKER

BROUGHT A LITTLE PIECE OF ITALY TO TEXAS!

My Texas post is: President, JEFCO Development, Houston, TX.

I came into this world on: April 30, 1962—the same birthday as Texas country singer icon Willie Nelson.

I was born & raised in: Born in Bryan, raised in Houston and Pearland, TX. I finished high school at La Chataigneraie, The International School of Geneva, Switzerland.

I hang my hat in: Houston, TX in Greenway Plaza just around the corner from the Compaq Center where the Houston Rockets play.

I'm a real cowboy because: In recreating the Doge's Palace in TX, I replaced the Lady of Venice with the Six Flags of Texas!

If you run into my friend Steve Flemma ask him about the time: We decided that more cowboys have been hurt after saying these words: "Hey Bubba, watch this!"

If you walked a mile in my boots: You'd stay the heck out of the computer business.

I love Texas because: Being from Texas, I get to remind people from New York they have a funny accent!

"How `bout ya?"

(pronounced "How `bout cha")

— Jim's Favorite Texas Saying

"His current dream is . . . modeled after the Doge's Palace in Venice, complete with canals, gondolas, waterfalls . . ."

I asked Jimmy Jongebloed to write my "Tall Texas Tale" because: *There are few people in life that exhibit such sincere honesty, as well as a fantastic zest for life. He has the ability to follow his heart on things other people wouldn't believe are attainable. And besides—he's the only one who can keep up with me!*

BTB Be the Ball
Productions, Inc.

Dear Martana:

    Each of us in our travels through life comes in contact with thousands of people. We remember only a small percentage of those we meet and still fewer become part of our lives. If you get the chance to meet Jimmy Fisher, you will undoubtedly never forget him, and he will likely become your friend.

    Hours after I met Jimmy, I felt like I had known him for years. It is easy to find a common ground with him, because he experiences life on so many different levels. At the time of our first conversation (which lasted nearly four hours), Jimmy was closing a real estate development deal with Office Depot, starting up another one with I-HOP, finalizing a record deal with Doug Supernaw for his new label Tack Records, raising money for the children's charity My Friends (in which he serves as a member of the board), and was preparing for his 8-year-old daughter to throw out the first ball at the next Astros home game!

    When I made the jump from the practice of law to the precarious world of filmaking, it was difficult for people to understand why I would make such a move. Jimmy was someone that understood perfectly, because it is all about following your dreams, which he has done all of his life. He has more passion for life than does anyone that I have ever met, and the energy he exudes spreads like a wildfire to the people around him.

    His current dream is the retail project called Portofino which, at a cost of $75 million, is the most lavish undertaking to date of his JEFCO Development Corp. This 650,000 square foot complex is modeled after the Doge's Palace in Venice, complete with canals, gondolas, waterfalls and a 120-foot recreation of the St. Marcos Bell Tower. To enter this "little piece of Italy in Texas" off of I-45 just outside of Houston, you have to turn onto a street that he named Alexandra after his precious daughter. Of course, this massive undertaking is not enough to hold the attention of this kinetic entrepreneur as he has just inked a deal to design and build the retail and hotel space for a theme park resort in Niagara Falls, Canada.

    Jimmy's business and personal projects have always been demanding and challenging, but over the past year he was faced with the most onerous and important task of his life – supporting his new wife, Leah, in her battle with cancer. He approached this challenge as he had everything he cares deeply about, with optimism, faith and love. The couple set an immediate wedding date upon learning of the disease, planning the ceremony and reception in less than two weeks, so that they could be together as husband and wife for the fight ahead. After extensive chemotherapy and undeniable courage, Leah is cancer free, and Jimmy is back to concentrating on his friends, family and projects at hand. Stay tuned – more dreams are on the way.

Sincerely,

Jimmy Jongebloed

6355 Westheimer, Suite 196, Houston, Texas 77057
Phone: (713)660-0039 Mobile: (713)582-4888 Fax: (713)781-0090

PAT GREEN
TRUBADOR DE TEJAS

WILLIE NELSON PLAYED ON MY FIFTH RECORD & I PLAYED HIS GUITAR "TRIGGER"!

My Texas post is: The Pat Green Band, Austin, TX.

I came into this world on: April 5th, 1972. I came out pickin' & grinnin' and I ain't stopped yet!

I was born & raised in: Born in San Antonio, TX, and raised in the little-known Central Texas metropolis of Bosqueville, TX, population 384 (including livestock).

I hang my hat in: Austin, TX.

I'm a real cowboy because: I've driven across the state to see a Willie Nelson concert and wound up sleeping in the bed of a pick-up with a beer bottle as a pillow.

If you run into my friend Brad Boozer, former Philadelphia Eagle, ask him: How high he'll let me press the bet on the 18th hole. Let's just say I made his house payment for a couple of months!

If you walked a mile in my boots: You'd better give my boots back—I don't care where you went!

I love Texas because: A long neck still goes a long way with the ladies!

"At all costs, live it up!"

— Pat's Favorite Texas Saying

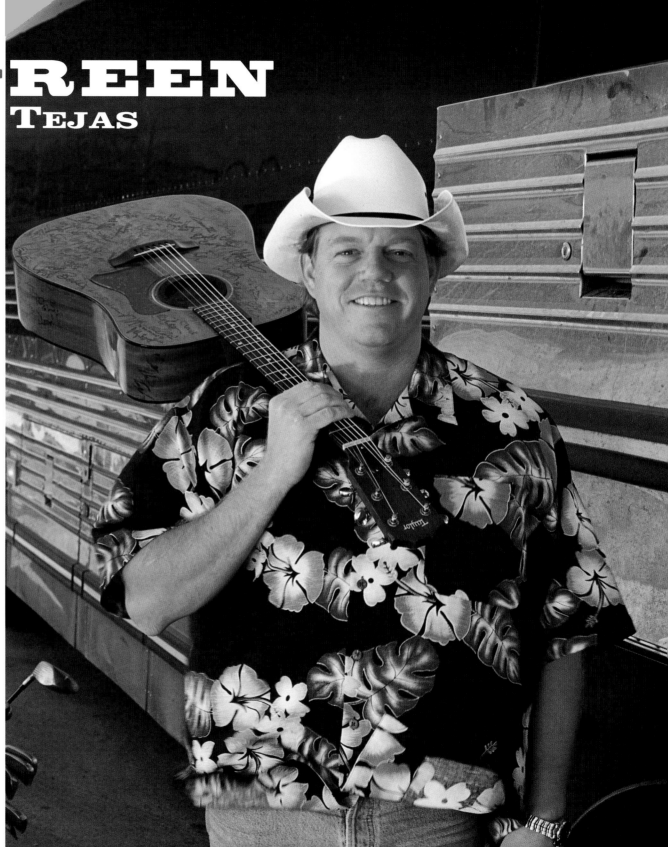

> "He sings of the joys and longings that a new generation of young Texans are expressing."

I asked Jerry Jeff Walker to write my "Tall Texas Tale" **because:** *He opened the door for me in this business, and I'm fairly certain I owe him my career (or at least my first born)!*

Austin, Texas

Dear Martana:

My first thoughts about Pat are that he's a young man with a good heart and strong will and also a very talented songwriter.

In the true tradition of Texas songwriters, he has learned what those before him have sung about, and he is creating on top of that. He sings of the joys and longings that a new generation of young Texans are expressing.

Pat reflects in his songs about growing up in Waco and those images he holds dear. (And we know he likes to drink beer.)

In an era when country music is using a "cookie cutter" formula for churning out its stars, Pat is unique. He has not waited for some record company executive to say, "It's your turn." He's doing it now – his own way. He is making his own records and selling them directly to his fans. That shows a lot of strength and character, and it says that he's in it for the long run.

Pat is also a very dynamic performer giving it his all each and every time he plays. He hasn't waited for someone else to tell him how to do it. He's just doing it and doing it extremely well.

I wish him all the best and great success.

Keep it in the short grass, Pat.

Jerry Jeff Walker

P.O. Box 39   Austin, Texas 78767   (512) 477-0036   Fax: (512) 477-0095

KELBY D. HAGAR
21ST-CENTURY GROCER

GROCERYWORKS.COM™
Your Friendly Neighborhood *Online* Grocer™

GARY J. FERNANDES
Chairman and Chief Executive Officer

June 20, 2000

Dear Martana:

About the worst thing anyone could say about a Texan is that he is "all hat, no cattle". Kelby Hagar is, metaphorically speaking, the exact opposite. Here is a guy who has achieved more in his thirty years than anyone I know in Texas, and that covers a lot of folks.

One of the characteristics of a Texas tale is its improbability, and certainly Kelby's story meets this test with a twist – it's true. Let me tell you what I mean. What could be more improbable than a young fellow from Hereford, Texas (where is that anyways?) leaving town to find his fame and fortune, but getting confused and going to San Angelo instead. Attending college in "The Cowtown on the Concho" and graduating three and a half years later with summa cum laude honors (whatever that is), a CPA certificate (I know what that is) and a bus ticket to Harvard. I am not sure that his Hereford/San Angelo/Harvard routing is one of a kind, but I'll bet there aren't many others who have ridden that particular trail.

Having read the law and seen the bright lights of Boston, Kelby regained his senses and returned to Dallas to hang out his shingle and commenced helping our corporate citizens dodge the tax man. This improbable story could end here and still get a few winks and nods at the café on the square in Hereford, but doesn't. Kelby, like many of our Texas forefathers, decided to explore a new frontier – a frontier not populated by mesquite trees and rattlesnakes, but by webmasters, servers, and other icons of cyberspace.

Talk about courage! What other macho Texas man do you know who would conceive a company for a market that didn't yet exist and make his corporate icon a bunch of dancing Bermuda onions?

It's hard to tell where this story might go from here. The company he founded, GroceryWorks.com, is on the front lines of internet wars and has already won several cyber skirmishes. I suspect that his story has no end, but that the highpoints along the way will be as improbable but true as its beginning. Like many of our other Texas business pioneers, Kelby validates the notion that "if you get up early and work hard, good things are bound to happen".

Sincerely,

Gary J. Fernandes

Gary J. Fernandes

14001 N. DALLAS PARKWAY • SUITE M100 • DALLAS, TEXAS • 75240
PHONE: 972-813-4065 • FAX: 972-813-4093
gfernandes@groceryworks.com

> "What other macho Texas man … would … make his corporate icon a bunch of dancing Bermuda onions?"

I asked Gary Fernandes to write my "Tall Texas Tale" because: *He writes my paycheck and he was the only one crazy enough to join me in building GroceryWorks.*

Founder of One of the First On-Line Grocery Stores— GroceryWorks.com

My Texas post is: Founder and President of GroceryWorks.com, 2727 Realty Road, Dallas, TX—take a left at the walk-in cooler.

I came into this world on: June 17, 1970— with more hair than I have now.

I was born & raised in: Hereford, TX, beef capitol of the world.

I hang my hat in: Dallas, TX, where you might see me making deliveries in one of our famous "fun fruit" trucks.

I'm a real cowboy because: I don't just eat quiche—I deliver it.

If you run into my friend Brent Dunn ask him about the time: We tried to re-heat pizza in the pizza box. We nearly burned down our rent house!

If you walked a mile in my boots: Your boots would be covered in white plastic booties. (We wear them to keep our customers' carpets clean during grocery deliveries.)

I love Texas because: It's the kind of place you can dream BIG and watch it come true.

"I like to give my employees a lot of rope, but I hold on tight to that rope."

— Kelby's Favorite Texas Saying

DANIEL K. HAGOOD
TRIAL LAWYER

CHAIRMAN AND FOUNDING PARTNER OF FITZPATRICK, HAGOOD, FISHER & HOLMES, P.C. —A TOP TEXAS TRIAL FIRM SPECIALIZING IN CRIMINAL & CIVIL LITIGATION

My Texas post is: Fitzpatrick, Hagood, Fisher & Holmes, P.C. –Dallas, TX.

I came into this world on: A sunny March day during Ike's administration.

I hang my hat in: Dallas, TX with my friends, partners and loyal dogs—Jakes and Jessie.

I'm a real cowboy because: I once rode a bronc in a rodeo—that horse was so mean, he is probably still kicking.

If you run into my friend Knox Fitzpatrick ask him about the time I: Was serving with the U.S. Marines in Saudi Arabia during Operation Desert Storm and Texas Governor Bill Clements appointed me as an "Admiral in the Texas Navy."

If you walked a mile in my boots: You would find that often there really are two sides to every story.

My ultimate Texas date would be: With the girl who is my other half—since a gentleman never talks, I will not reveal her identity but she knows who she is.

I love Texas because: It's a place where courage, integrity and hard work are valued and rewarded.

"No guts, no glory."

— Daniel's Favorite Texas Saying

◀◀◀ BOON-CHAPMAN

Ms. Martana Hanson, Publisher   February 10, 2000
TEXAS MEN
25 Highland Park Village, Suite 100-140
Dallas, Texas 75205

Dear Martana:

I first met Dan in the mid 80's while working with him in the Dallas County District Attorney's Office and I knew immediately that he is a true Texan. He is smart as hell, tough, fearless and loyal. I never saw a better lawyer in a courtroom. He has never lost a death penalty case and, in the first civil case he tried after entering private practice, he turned $11,000 of damages into a million-dollar verdict for his client. Juries like and follow him and opponents fear him. Let me share with you a few examples of what I am talking about.

We once tried a multi-defendant drug case in Emory, Texas, population 818. Intrigue and a sense of danger surrounded the trial. Death threats were leveled against Dan and myself, the Judge and witnesses. The town was scared -- Dan was not. He set about winning the trial in the courtroom and demonstrating, outside the courtroom, that there was nothing to fear. He was more than a trial lawyer -- he was like the white-hatted Sheriff come to town to establish law and order. His fearlessness and easy good humor was contagious and soon the town was won over. By the time he won the trial, some four and one half months later, I bet he could have been elected mayor if he had wanted this.

In another case he handled after entering private practice, Dan represented Terry Brown in his high profile capital murder case. The Richardson, Texas police department seemingly had an airtight case against Mr. Brown with two separate confessions and plenty of physical evidence. Soon after they filed this case, Richardson itself was sued in federal court for a multi-million dollar wrongful death claim. Richardson then asked Dan to represent them, despite the fact he was against them in Mr. Brown's case. After obtaining Mr. Brown's consent, Dan agreed to do so. The result -- the charges against both Brown and Richardson were dismissed with prejudice!! Dan's skill and integrity in the handling of these cases distinguished him as one of Texas' best trial lawyers.

Finally, I must mention Dan's service to our country. He is a U.S. Marine infantry officer with the rank of Colonel, United States Marine Corps Reserve. During Operation Desert Storm, Dan was serving with a reserve unit that was unlikely to be called to active duty. So, like a true Texan, Dan volunteered for combat duty and left the safety of his home to go to Saudi Arabia. He could have remained safe and sound in the U.S., but for him the right thing to do was volunteer -- that's about as Texan as you can get!

Texas is lucky to have him as one of its citizens and I'm lucky to call him my friend.

Kevin

Kevin Chapman
President

7600 Chevy Chase Drive / P.O. Box 9201 / Austin, Texas 78766 / (512) 454-2681

I asked Kevin Chapman to write my "Tall Texas Tale" because: *He is a great friend who knows me both as a trial attorney and as a Colonel, United States Marine Corps Reserve.*

"He was more than a trial lawyer -- he was like the white-hatted Sheriff come to town to establish law and order."

JOHN D. HARKEY, JR.
INVESTOR, ENTREPRENEUR & ADVENTURER

CREATING A BILLION-DOLLAR RESTAURANT HOLDING COMPANY FROM A COLLEGE BUSINESS PARTNERSHIP!

My Texas post is: Chairman of Consolidated Restaurant Companies, Inc. and Managing Partner of Cracken, Harkey, Street & Hartnett, L.L.C. in Dallas, TX.

I was born & raised in: Born in San Antonio, TX and raised in Brownwood, TX.

I hang my hat in: Highland Park and as often as possible at the Black Jack— my ranch in Katemcy, TX.

I came into this world on: September 12, 1960, while my dad was in conversation outside the room with President John F. Kennedy and Lyndon B. Johnson!

I'm a real cowboy because: I am a fifth-generation Texan and learned the art of Texas business from my father, a fourth-generation rancher, who still owns a farm and ranch wholesale supply company.

If you run into my friend John Cracken ask him about the time: He surprised me on my birthday by arranging a speaking role for me in a Universal Studios movie.

If you walked a mile in my boots: You would run across my family, friends and Texas-size challenges.

I love Texas because: Of its historic spirit. No matter where you travel in the world, Texans and Texas exude a rare combination of adventure, friendliness and endless optimism. It is extremely contagious and I miss Texas when I'm away.

"What's most important in life is finding a game worth playing."

— John's Favorite Texas Saying

Dear Martana,

It gives me great pleasure to write on behalf of John Harkey, because he reflects the true spirit of Texas. When you first meet John, his intelligence, energy, creativity and Texas charm are immediately apparent. Looking further, his style and sophistication might lead you to believe he grew up in the city, but after a few minutes, a slight Central Texas accent hints of deeper rural roots. Like me, John was raised in Brownwood, and just like me, John has worked hard to achieve success. Even though we grew up in the same hometown, I never had the opportunity to know John until we met in Dallas in 1990 (perhaps because I am 20 years older). Yet we both still share the same small town values forged at an early age by loving parents—honesty, integrity and determination—which helped develop the incredible work ethic we both possess.

John's desire to excel first led him to the University of Texas at Austin where he played golf before concentrating on academics. After graduating from the UT Business Honors Program, he continued his pursuit of higher education at UT Law School, completing his JD after transferring to Stanford University, where he received his MBA. Before returning to Texas, John polished and enhanced his unique diversity and breadth of business experience by living and working in New York, Boston and London.

Along the way John built many long-lasting friendships. As a matter of fact, he met John Cracken while attending UT and of course, that friendship evolved into the 20-year business partnership of Cracken & Harkey, L.L.P. which in turn generated Cracken, Harkey, Street & Co., L.L.C. and then Cracken, Harkey, Street & Hartnett, L.L.C.

As Chairman of our holding company, Consolidated Restaurant Companies, Inc., John developed and coordinated the strategic vision behind our consolidation strategy. Over the last two years, our team has built a regional restaurant powerhouse with 152 restaurants in 21 states and Canada with over 8,000 dedicated employees. His leadership has diversified our holding company into four restaurant platforms that includes ownership of historic Texas brands—El Chico Restaurants, Inc., Spaghetti Warehouse Restaurants, Inc., Good Eats Holding Co., Inc. and Cool River Restaurants, Inc. We feed 25,000,000 people per year. John has also consistently proven his exceptional ability to recognize and create value in a broad number of industries and investments. Most recently, he has backed several successful technology and Internet ventures.

John is a true Texas adventurer at heart. His fast pace life includes auto-racing, mountain climbing, snow skiing and hunting adventures. An Eagle Scout in his youth, John continues to honor early service commitments to the community by serving as a new board member of the Circle Ten Boy Scouts Board of Directors and other charities.

I have been fortunate to have the opportunity to build a successful company with John and lay the foundation for a billion dollar restaurant consolidation. It has truly been a great pleasure for me to be a partner with him and have him as my friend. He never lets grass grow under his feet. You'll be certain to hear more of him in the near future.

Sincerely,

Gene Street

CRC CONSOLIDATED RESTAURANT COMPANIES, INC.   12200 STEMMONS FREEWAY   DALLAS, TEXAS 75234

"We feed 25,000,000 people per year."

I asked Gene Street to write my "Tall Texas Tale" because:

Gene Street is Texas Big! His reputation as a restaurateur is legendary, but to me his character is his greatest strength.

JON HENDRICKS
PRINTER OF FINE EATIN' & DRINKIN' THINGS

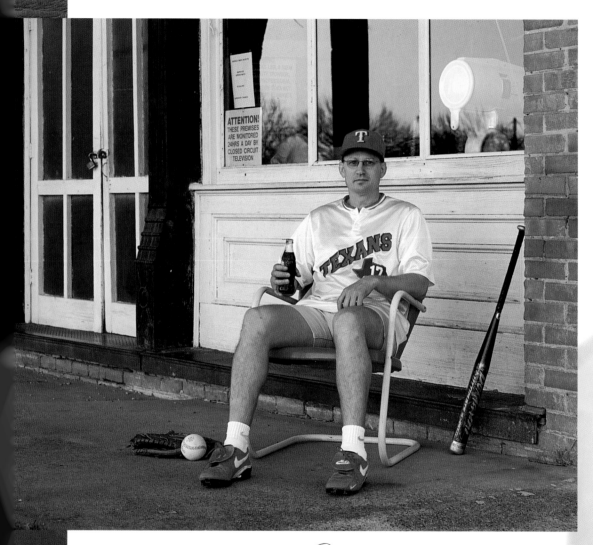

ATTENDED THOUSANDS OF CELEBRATIONS & NEVER LEFT MY CHAIR!

My Texas post is: President, Fabsco Inc. in Dallas, TX where we print and stamp napkins, coasters, playing cards, stationary, cups, and lots of fun items for celebrations.

I came into this world on: December 16, 1957.

I was born & raised in: Anna, TX. I went to school in the same building as my parents and grandmother.

I hang my hat in: Anna, TX, where we all know and help each other.

I'm a real cowboy because: I'm a legend in my own mind!

If you run into my friend Mike Huggins ask him about the time: We were arguing over a girl. We stopped on a bridge and rolled dice in the headlights to see who got to ask that little filly out first.

If you walked a mile in my boots: You'd be huntin' for a mule!

My ultimate Texas date would be: To go to a track meet in Austin, then a baseball game, and then a hockey game. If there is still time, we'd go for dinner too!

I love Texas because: It's big enough to have coastline, woods, mountains, canyons, desert and a wide diversity of people.

"Don't worry about the horse, just load the wagon."

— Jon's Favorite Texas Saying

Bramcon
CONSTRUCTION CO.

February 18, 2000

Dear Martana,

When I married my wife April, I had no idea what an added bonus I would receive in the person of my brother-in-law, Jon Hendricks: my good friend, business partner and confidant.

At the age of 21, he became a city councilman in his hometown and after serving two two-year terms he became one of the youngest Mayors in the State of Texas. He threw himself into his job with the exuberance and dedication he shows in everything he does. He implemented a new computer accounting system and new water billing system and also sold bonds to upgrade the water and sewer systems.

He is a member of many boards and organizations that help promote programs for the youth as well as the city. He recently initiated a one-half cent sales tax election to help promote the city as well as build new parks for the youth of Anna. He is always there to help in any way he can - even picking up trash after baseball games.

When my wife April bought Marj's / Fabsco it was just a retail store with a small wholesale operation in the back. She asked Jon to come in to help her with structuring the business. At the time he was involved in two other companies and could only give a limited amount of time. As time passed, both Marj's and Fabsco were growing at such a pace that more and more of their time was required. As the demands on both of them grew April offered Jon a partnership which he gladly accepted. With April's extraordinary product development and marketing skills and Jon's business sense and eye for detail, they became a perfect business match!

Time will prove the both of them a force to be reckoned with. Just keep your eyes on Marj's Stationers and Fabsco, Inc. – you haven't seen anything yet!

Sincerely,

Mike Bosworth

7807 Caruth Court • Dallas, Texas 75225 • 214.361.2283 • Fax 214.361.2083

" ... he became one of the youngest Mayors in the State of Texas."

I asked Mike Bosworth to write my "Tall Texas Tale" because: *He can shoot the bull and tell stories with the best of `em but he's my brother-in-law, so I won't put much stock in his tale!*

BILLY HICKS
PRO-SPORTS FRANCHISOR

FOUNDED TWO CHAMPIONSHIP TEAMS— THE LONDON MONARCHS OF NFL EUROPE & THE DALLAS BURN OF MAJOR LEAGUE SOCCER

My Texas post is: Founding President and General Manager of the Dallas Burn Soccer team in our uptown headquarters, and watching the team play from the press box of the Cotton Bowl and now Founding Executive of the XFL.

I hang my hat in: Dallas, TX, a field of dreams.

I came into this world on: October 25, 1960, with a play list.

I'm a real cowboy because: The simple pleasures make me happiest—a good sunset, a good meal, a good song and good company.

If you run into one of my friends ask them about my: Secret passion to be a rock n' roll star. They'll tell you I love to sing and play the guitar for friends or anyone who will listen!

If you walked a mile in my boots: Your feet would hurt, because I inherited bad feet and my favorite boots from my grandfather.

I love Texas because: Of chips & salsa, Shiner Bock Pale, Jerry Jeff Walker and the friendliest people in the world.

"Work hard, play harder, sleep good."

— Billy's Favorite Texas Saying

D A L L A S B U R N

2602 McKinney Avenue, Suite 200 • Dallas, TX 75204 • 214.979.0303 • 214.979.1118 Fax
www.burnsoccer.com

When Billy Hicks hired me to be the head coach of the Dallas Burn in 1996, I assumed that this was a guy with an extensive background in soccer. I figured that he had probably played collegiately and possibly dabbled a bit in the professional leagues. I mean Major League Soccer was entrusting this guy to build a franchise from scratch – he'd have to have played the game, right? Wrong. Billy came out to one of our first practices ever. Since not all the players had reported to camp yet, we were short a few guys. No problem, I'll just stick Billy out there. Well, that's when I came to know what soccer skills (or lack thereof) that he possessed. I told Billy to mark Leonel Alvarez, a ferocious competitor who just happened to also play on the Colombian National Team. Billy did a bang up job – until Leonel actually got the ball. With Billy standing in front of him, Leonel calmly slipped the ball through Billy's legs as if Billy were simply a croquet wicket. Billy had just been nutmegged – the ultimate insult for a defender. No big deal, I thought, he just hasn't played in a while. The next time Leonel got the ball, it was apparent that Billy wasn't going to let Leonel through again. In fact, as Leonel reared back to blast a shot, Billy stood his ground. As the ball met Billy's face with a sickening thud, he was done for the day. We later found out, as if his on-field exploits didn't already prove it, but Billy had never played a minute of soccer in his life. In fact, we came to find out that Billy had been a football guy all his life, spending many years working for the National Football League. Needless to say, the decision was made that day never to put Billy in that position again. That decision worked just fine with both me and Billy until the day that the English rock group Def Leppard came to town. It seems that the boys in the band were itching for a pick-up game of soccer and challenged the Burn staff. No problem, I thought, there are plenty of guys in the Burn office that play soccer. So we fielded a nice little team and set out to show these guys that the Americans can play a "foreign" sport. The game was a defensive battle with neither team able to break through. In fact, the one-armed drummer from Def Leppard was giving us fits. No one could get by him. With about five minutes left in the game, our forward was so frustrated by the one-armed defender that he was mentally not even in the game. I knew that a change had to be made. I looked down our team bench and realized that we had no substitutes. The only person on the sidelines besides me was none other than Billy Hicks. I turned to Billy and told him that this was his chance to redeem himself on the soccer field. This wasn't just a game, I told him. This was the USA vs. Europe. I instructed Billy to go in at forward and to try and distract the one-armed defender. I thought maybe this would free up someone else and give us the opportunity to score. With just a few minutes remaining in the game, Billy trotted onto the field. His first few minutes on the field were uneventful as our players obeyed my instructions by keeping the ball away from Billy. Remember, he was just out there as a distraction. But, with one minute left in the match, the ball caromed Billy's way. Billy apparently decided he was going to try to take the ball to goal himself. Yes, the same Billy that was still wondering why we played with a round ball instead of an oblong one. He got the ball and the one-armed defender was closing in fast. No one had gotten by him yet and I really held no hope that Billy would be the first. In an attempt to dribble the ball towards the goal, Billy stepped on the ball instead, almost sending him to the ground. He inexplicably maintained his balance and kept possession of the ball. The one-armed defender, not having the greatest balance with only one arm, was so thrown off by Billy's wild maneuvering that he got caught leaning the wrong way. When he tried to go the other way, he lost his balance and hit the ground, leaving Billy one-on-one with the goalkeeper. Billy pushed the ball forward and, with the goalie closing fast, reared back and blasted the ball into the net just before time expired. In his exuberance, Billy ripped off his shirt (proving to us all that he spends far too much time in the office) and went racing down the field in a wild celebration. The NFL guy had propelled us to victory.

Dave Dir
Dave Dir
Dallas Burn Head Coach

US OPEN CUP
Champions
1997

> " . . . the boys in the [Def Leppard] band were itching for a pick-up game of soccer and challenged the Burn staff."

I asked Coach Dir to write my "Tall Texas Tale" because: *When I asked him we were on a six-game winning streak and I knew he would be upbeat and funny!*

AL G. HILL, JR.
CONSUMMATE ENTREPRENEUR

"Al is the eldest grandson of the legendary H.L. Hunt of East Texas oil field fame."

I asked Senator Kay Bailey Hutchison to write my "Tall Texas Tale" because: *She is an idol of mine. Kay personifies the qualities that make Texas the great state that it is.*

KAY BAILEY HUTCHISON
UNITED STATES SENATOR

February 29, 2000

Dear Martana:

The Great State of Texas and its native citizens are well defined by many outstanding characteristics: heritage, courage, individualism, determination, patriotism, entrepreneurialism and self-reliance, as well as the ability to create and/or carry forward a legacy.

Texas born Al G. Hill, Jr., personifies many of these Texas qualities that are clearly intertwined in most aspects of his life. Al is the eldest grandson of the legendary H.L. Hunt of East Texas oil field fame.

The dedication Al has shown to helping elect conservative and responsible people to political office is also typified by his service and active, caring involvement on the boards of Southern Methodist University and the Baylor Medical Center in Dallas. Along with his mother and two sisters, Al was honored as the Family of The Year in 2000 by the YWCA for their outstanding contributions to the Dallas community.

Being born and raised in the cosmopolitan Texas city of Dallas, Al was not a rancher, but became an international citizen as a player on the tennis tour and then went on to co-found World Championship Tennis of which he was president for twenty-three years. WCT operated thousands of professional tennis tournaments in over 100 cities, with offices in New York, Detroit, Tokyo, London and, of course, headquartered in Big D. Every year, from every corner of the world, the media and fans converged on Dallas for the prestigious WCT Finals, telecast into over 42 countries. WCT caused "the tennis boom" and it is fair to say that albeit inadvertently, it inspired millions of people to take up the game of tennis and consequently begin moving their bodies toward better health.

A dedicated family man, Al's mother, his three children and two sisters live within a few blocks of each other and spend much of their time together in civic affairs and business activities. They also have a monthly family meeting to discuss their goals and progress.

When flights leave for London, Paris, Rio de Janeiro, Tokyo or even Canada and Mexico, you can watch for Al, unless he is headed somewhere on his own Hawker Jet or hovering over the DFW Metroplex in his LongRanger helicopter.

Texas (and everywhere else) can use more people like Al who are dedicated to giving back to their community and state and striving to improve the world for other people. Al truly represents the soul and spirit of Texas!

Sincerely,

Kay Bailey Hutchison

Kay Bailey Hutchison

NOT PAID FOR AT GOVERNMENT EXPENSE

Co-Founded
World Championship Tennis (WCT)

My Texas post is: Texas Entrepreneur, Dallas, TX. Co-founder of several businesses including World Championship Tennis—which has transformed lives all over the world.

I came into this world on: An otherwise uneventful February morning on the 3rd.

I was born & raised in: Dallas, the most consistently vibrant city in the United States!

I hang my hat in: Park Cities on Exall Lake, in a house known well for its original Dallas icon owner of 63 years—Doctor Ed Carey.

I'm a real cowboy because: I would never want to live anywhere else other than Texas.

If you run into my friend Don Donnally ask him about the time: The butter on the light bulb at St. Mark's School of Texas was dripping on the desk of the teacher's pet student.

If you walked a mile in my boots: You would be dedicated to the state of Texas, its citizens and its compassionate organizations.

My ultimate Texas date would be: Whoever accompanies me to the swearing in ceremony of President George W. Bush.

I love Texas because: The state personifies the best there is . . . opportunities, values and caring about fellow human beings.

"When asked for advice always respond, 'It will be worth about what I charge and it's free.'"

— Al's Favorite Texas Saying

DR. JIM HILL
HORSE DOCTOR & BOOT MAKER

OWNED A RACEHORSE NAMED SEATTLE SLEW—A COLT WHO WON THE TRIPLE CROWN!

My Texas post is: J.B. Hill Boot Company, Ltd. in El Paso, TX—where we are dedicated to making the finest Benchmade, Hand Lasted Western boots in the World!

I came into this world on: March 15, 1938—the Ides of March (it's been good luck for me)!

I hang my hat in: El Paso, TX—when I am not at the racetrack.

I'm a real cowboy because: I am a Texas Bootmaker. The Cowboy boot is the only fashion statement that is truly American. The cowboy boot design evolved in the towns and villages of Texas cattle country.

If you run into my friend, boot designer, Ivan Holguin ask him why I: Got booted out of retirement and into the footwear industry. This business has more moving parts than an octopus—I never know which leg to pull first!

If you walked a mile in my boots: They would be real comfortable. And you'd have girls chasin' ya down the road—we sell some SEXY boots!

I love Texas because: The people here have beautiful "soles!"

"A well made boot is like any fine article of clothing. It fits your curves, feels right, gives joy, draws compliments."

— Jim's Favorite Texas Saying

"To hear this story, you'd think a man could go to the auction, buy one cheap horse, and make a whole career out of it!"

I asked Ed Bowen to write my "Tall Texas Tale" because: *Ed's the only writer I know who writes almost exclusively about horses and horse people, but he's never been to Texas!*

GRAYSON - JOCKEY CLUB RESEARCH FOUNDATION, INC.

821 CORPORATE DRIVE • LEXINGTON, KY 40503

606-224-2850
FAX (606) 224-2853

Dear Martana:

Long before my friend Dr. Jim Hill moved down to Texas and made something substantial of himself in the boot business, he used to come around Kentucky horse sales. Gradually, there built up this legend that was so darned exaggerated sounding that when we tried to sell the story to Hollywood they just laughed. I was told by a producer, "You'll see a full-length feature about ants before you'll see a movie as crazy sounding as that Jim Hill story."

Anyway, here's the tale on Jim: About 25 years ago, he was a young veterinarian who just a few years earlier had graduated from fishing for catfish down in Lake Okechobee, Florida. He came around Kentucky with a little money, and while he and a young fellow from the Northwest got into a kicking match with a recalcitrant newspaper vending machine they got to talking. First thing you know, they and their wives got into a race horse partnership.

Later, they were down here again at a yearling sale and bought this colt for $17,000. That's not chump change, but it sure doesn't get you much in the way of pedigree fashion in the Thoroughbred business. Somehow the story got out that this was the same colt that got named Seattle Slew and became the only horse in history to go through the Triple Crown---Kentucky Derby, Preakness, and Belmont Stakes---while still undefeated. Well, that's a pretty tall tale, but even that wasn't enough. Next thing you know, the story gets embellished----the horse almost dies, but then is brought back to health to be a champion again the next year. Then he goes off to stud and, wham, he's turning out so many great runners that a single share in the horse is said to be worth $1 million. And old Jim's right there taking in his share of all the stud fees while at the same time racing some of Seattle Slew's best runners himself.

To hear this story, you'd think a man could go to the auction, buy one cheap horse, and make a whole career out of it!

Well, the most startling thing about this story is that it was all absolutely true. I was a racing reporter at the time and watched it unfold moment by moment. Couldn't believe it then; can hardly believe it now, but it was the truth.

Jim and his wife Sally did a lot for the horse business, helped with horse health research, etc., and I know he's turning out quality boots for his fellow Texans. I do take umbrage at his telling you that I've never been to Texas, though. That's blasphemy about a man who's eaten chicken-fried steak from Elgin to Amarillo. I once even visited Bill Hobby in his Lt. Governor's office, and I was man enough not to shield my eyes against that bright silver belt buckle of his.

All the best,

Ed Bowen

BOB HOPKINS
FUNDRAISER EXTRAORDINAIRE

FOUNDER OF PHILANTHROPY IN TEXAS MAGAZINE

My Texas post is: Where I raise awareness about charitable activities across Texas as the Founder and President of a fundraising consulting company and *Philanthropy in Texas* magazine in Dallas, TX.

I hang my hat in: The Swiss Avenue Historic District of Dallas, TX.

I came into this world on: September 6, 1943—on the go.

I'm a real cowboy because: I have a ranch, horses and barbed-wire.

If you run into my friend Marla ask her about the time I: Lost my car. At the Shelton School, a school for learning different children, where I served as Director of Development from 1984-87, it was brought to my attention that my attention might be deficit disordered! One day, I drove to the grocery store, parked three blocks away from my office and then walked back. An hour later I went to get my car to go to a meeting and found NO car. Panicked, I called the police, who found it at the grocery store where I had left it. Just a small example of my life!

If you walked a mile in my boots: You'd be tired.

I love Texas because: Of the charitable attitude.

"It's a great life, if you don't weaken."

— Bob's Favorite Texas Saying

Carolyn Farb

Dear Martana,

Bob Hopkins is a rising star, cowboy and *publisher* all in one! His energy, ideas and skills in the art of fundraising have earned him the reputation of a *can-do* fundraising executive. Bob has raised funds for many non-profit organizations including the Shelton School, the Texas Neurofibromatosis Foundation, SUN & STAR 1996 and many other worthwhile causes.

In 1996, Bob began his dream, *Philanthropy In Texas*, a magazine about Texans and their spirit of giving. The magazine highlights the rewards of charitable giving, in addition to providing invaluable knowledge and a forum in which to share information. The success of the publication has encouraged Bob to create similar magazines in major cities across the country. He is constantly thinking of innovative and creative ways to enhance the public's view of philanthropy

At the top of Bob's list of many interests and passions is his love of horses. He is the proud owner of several Arabians - *Ali Baba*, *Cricket* and her filly, *Sherrye Rochesta*. He spends what little free time he has on his land just south of Dallas riding off into the sunset. On occasion, he joins other cowboys and cowgirls for charitable trail rides. With Bob, there is never a dull moment.

When working at Shelton, a special school for children with learning challenges, Bob realized that he could have used the Shelton approach when he was growing up. His friends had noticed that he exhibited behavior attributed to attention deficit disorder. They realized he was like an absent minded professor always searching for his car keys or sometimes even his car. On one occasion, he forgot to make the special arrangements for a $10,000 donor who patiently waited for a car that was promised but never arrived.

Bob makes a difference in the lives of all the people he has reached through his dedication. With boundless energy, he inspires confidence in others to follow their dreams. Keeping up with Bob is no small feat. He is a true "Texas Man".

My Best,

Carolyn

Carolyn Farb

"With boundless energy, he inspires confidence in others to follow their dreams."

I asked Carolyn Farb to write my "Tall Texas Tale" because: *I admire her creative mind and her generous spirit.*

STEVE JONG
VICE-PRESIDENT TO DISHWASHER

PROVED THAT MOO GOO GAI PAN AND PEACH COBBLER GO TOGETHER LIKE TEXAS MEN & COWBOY BOOTS!

My Texas post is: Greeting our customers at one of our ten area Ming Garden, Ming's Express, or Manchu Wok locations or . . . on my cell phone talking to people about opening up more restaurants or about the best home-based business—Excel Communications.

I came into this world on: January 15, 1962—cookin' and a chattin'.

I hang my hat in: Plano, TX—"A Fortunate Choice."

I'm a real cowboy because: I don't mind doing the dirty work.

If you run into my friend Roland Hernandez ask him about the time we: Drove his Jeep into the lake. We were supposed to take a right turn and we took a left, grazed a couple of trees, and ended up in about 28 feet of water. Everything turned out all right though—we were able to save the cassettes and the ice chest!

If you walked a mile in my boots: You would have picked up over one million dirty dishes and then kept on going with the next dirty dish!

I love Texas because: You see people from every walk of life.

"It's about working smarter, not harder."

— Steve's Favorite Texas Saying

"... and announced in a deep, Southern drawl, "Hah, ah'm Steve. Y'all's order's here."

I asked Carol Thompson to write my "Tall Texas Tale" because: *Her perception is the same as everybody else's about me: "laid back, Asian-Cajun, country, country"!*

June 1, 1998

Dear Martana:

I'll never forget the first time I met Steve Jong. It was lunch time, and everyone at the office was in the mood for something different. We decided on Chinese food from Ming Garden, and called in our To Go order. Thirty minutes later, a nice, smartly dressed Oriental young man walked in with our order, and announced in a deep, Southern drawl, "Hah, ah'm Steve. Y'all's order's here. Where d'ya want me to put it?" My initial reaction was to giggle, but I somehow held it in. I've met numerous American-born Chinese people before, but none with such a pronounced accent. It just struck me as humorous at the time. But Steve will attest to the fact that he has the same effect on almost everyone he meets. Anyway, his accent wasn't the only thing about Steve that made an impression. This polite, gregarious young man proceeded to neatly unload our lunch on the breakroom table. Upon presentation of the bill, I attempted to give him the standard 20% tip, which he graciously declined. I was somewhat puzzled, as I've never known a delivery person to turn down a tip. So I tried again, and he declined again. Giving up, I then thanked him, and he left.

About two weeks later, I headed to Ming Garden with our account executive, Jennifer, who had set an appointment with the Vice President to discuss his advertising needs. We walked into the corporate office, and the first person we saw was the nice young man who had delivered our lunch. He was on the phone, taking a To Go order from a customer. After he'd finished his call, I greeted him, told him I remembered him, and asked to see the Vice President. His response was, "Y'all wait here. Aa'll go git him." He then exited to a side office. The next thing we heard was him shouting "Y'all come on in." So we did, only to find him sitting behind a desk, with no one else in the room but us. Confused, we asked where the Vice President was, at which point he said, "Yer lookin' at him." We walked out of that office with Ming Garden as a new account, and Steve Jong as a new friend.

After three years of knowing Steve, I can honestly say that for a person who has so much going for him, he couldn't be more humble. No task is too great, or menial for Steve to handle. Ask Steve and he'll tell you that "if you want your employees to give 200%, you've got to be willing to give it yourself. That means doing everything from sweeping the floors to delivering orders to customers. How can I expect them to do it if I won't do it myself?" With his rare modesty, down-home friendly attitude and Southern charm, Steve Jong is the epitome of a true Southern gentleman...with a little Oriental spice added for flavor. As a business person, he's honest, fair and straightforward. As a friend, he's one in a million. As a Texas man, you couldn't ask for a better candidate.

Sincerely,

Carol Thompson

Carol Thompson
President

AD CETERA, INC. • 5000 QUORUM DRIVE • SUITE 725 • DALLAS, TEXAS 75240 • 972/387-5577 • FAX 972/387-0034
www.adceterainc.com   info@adceterainc.com

JOHN JUSTIN
JUSTIN BOOTS, SECOND-GENERATION

CARRYING ON THE 120-YEAR-OLD FAMILY BUSINESS AS MY GRANDFATHER WISHED

My Texas post is: Justin Boots headquarters in Fort Worth, TX.

I came into this world on: January 17, 1917, boot scootin'.

I was born in: Nocona, TX and raised in Fort Worth, the home of the Fort Worth Stock Show.

I hang my hat in: Fort Worth, TX, where I love to rodeo!

I'm a cowboy at heart because: I've always loved the life of cowboys.

If you run into my friend Jim Shoulders ask him about the first time I: Rode one of his bulls. Jim got me to ride a big white bull named Buford T. Lite at a Justin party in Fort Worth, TX. Buford was a popular bull, known for making appearances at Texas bars. Showing up with Buford at the crowded party of thousands of people certainly got everyone's attention!

If you walked a mile in my boots: You'd be walking in Justin boots.

I love Texas because: I've always loved Texas and Texans buy cowboy boots!

"I've always loved the cowboys and the rodeo."

— John's Favorite Texas Saying

Rodeo's Champion of Champions

JIM SHOULDERS' ENTERPRIZES

J LAZY S RANCH

P. O. Box 819   ●   Henryetta, Oklahoma 74437-0819

JIM SHOULDERS
PH. 918-652-7582
HENRYETTA, OKLA.

Having known and been friends with John Justin Jr. longer than either of us want to admit (over 50 years) I have found him to be a loyal Texan and as hard as I've tried to get him to become an "Okie" his deep rooted loyalty remains a Texan.

Even though John wasn't ranch raised he has always been a Texas Cowboy.

Rodeo and the Fort Worth Stock Show have been almost as big a part of his life as Justin Company cowboy boots.   His Stock Show start was as a young usher in the old Northside Coliseum and he worked his way up to become Chairman of the Board where his influence helped raise millions of dollars to improve the Will Rogers complex into what is now the largest rodeo and livestock show in the United States with 30 performances.

Let me tell you how much John Justin loves rodeo.   When John married his lovely bride, Jane, they could have chosen any number of romantic, glamorous honeymoon places in the world.   Would you believe that after a brief trip to New Orleans they went to the Cheyenne Frontier Days Rodeo in Cheyenne, Wyoming.

John and Jane's rodeo parties became as famous as the rodeo at Fort Worth and all rodeo people have been Justin Boot Company customers for many years.

John was also a contestant at the Fort Worth Rodeo one time.   I must admit it was after one of Jane's famous parties where a small amount of "brave making beverages" had been served.   John and two World Champions (Reg Kesler and Jack Roddy) won the Wild Horse Race.   John said he wanted to retire a champion so he never entered again.

The Justin Boots Cowboy Crisis Fund program has been the biggest help ever to critcally injured contestants.   The program offers medical and financial support for their families while the Justin traveling Healer program helps injured contestants on the spot with medical attention from great doctors at no cost to the contestant.

As much as John contributed to rodeo he still had time to build Justin Companies into Texas' greatest industries including, Justin Boots, Tony Lama Boots, Nocona Boots, Chippewa, Acme Brick Co., Featherlite Building Products, American Tile Supply and Northland Publishing Co....all of this while serving on various boards of other Texas companies.

Texans always say that everything is "bigger and better" in Texas but this Oklahoman knows there will never be a better Texan nor a better man than John Justin Jr.

Jim Shoulders

Jim Shoulders

> " . . . as hard as I've tried to get him to become an 'Okie,' his deep rooted loyalty remains a Texan."

I asked Jim Shoulders to write my "Tall Texas Tale" because: *He knows me pretty well and he'd be afraid to not say something good!*

W. PARK KERR
TEXAS FOOD AMBASSADOR TO THE WORLD

THE EL PASO CHILE COMPANY CHANGED THE WAY AMERICA EATS!

My Texas post is: Founder and creative spirit of the El Paso Chile Company & Tequila Nacional in downtown El Paso, TX.

I came into this world: Too close to X-mas, 1958.

I was born & raised in: Suburban El Paso as a ninth-generation Texan!

I hang my hat in: My El Paso casa, over-looking three states and two countries.

I'm a real cowboy because: No hat, no horse, no ranch—but I know how to make the best damn chile and salsa on earth!

If you run into my brother-in-law and business partner ask him about the time: My mid-life crisis was in full swing. And instead of a blond, a corvette convertible and a face lift—I moved to Mexico and started distilling tequila.

If you walked a mile in my boots: Your tongue would be on fire and your heels would be chillin'.

I love Texas because: The food's hot and the people are cool!

"Don't dream it, be it!"

— Park's Favorite Texas Saying

"He grabbed my briefcase, we ran out of the building, and we didn't stop eating for two days."

I asked Pat Sharpe, <u>Texas Monthly</u> Food Editor, to write my "Tall Texas Tale" because: *She is the bravest fire-eater in the Republic of Texas . . . some like it hot . . . some like it hotter!*

TexasMonthly

Internet Web site: www.texasmonthly.com

P.O. Box 1569, Austin, TX 78767-1569
Phone (512) 320-6900 **Fax** (512) 476-9007

February 24, 2000

Park Kerr is a lot like a human tornado. You can either stand there in the path of destruction—well, enthusiasm—or be a willing part of the energy vortex. I've known him since the early eighties on a casual basis—a business call here and there. He is the founder and creative spirit of the El Paso Chile Company and the city of El Paso's unofficial booster, especially for anything concerning Hispanic culture. My business is writing about restaurants and food for *Texas Monthly,* so last year when I got the most insane story assignment of my career—find the 75 best Mexican restaurants in Texas and the neighboring border cities of Mexico—I knew I needed help. I called Park.

"Come to the office immediately when you get to town. I know exactly where you need to go." He was waiting for me in khaki shorts, a Hawaiian shirt, and running shoes, sort of bouncing on his toes: "How long can you stay? I hope you didn't eat anything on the plane. We'll go in my car." He grabbed my briefcase, we ran out of the building, and we didn't stop eating for two days. It turned out that Park knows every Mexican restaurant in El Paso, especially the little *taquerías* and holes-in-the-wall that we both love. We'd burst in, he would find the owner or manager (who was invariably a friend) and catch up on the latest gossip, and then we'd order about six entrées between the two of us.

By the time we got through eating a bite of this and a bite of that, the table would look like a land mine had exploded on it. With Park, nothing was ever just "OK." It was "the most" or "the best" or "the worst" or "the least": "This is the best *chile con queso* in the UNIVERSE!" Or "This stuff is DOGFOOD!" We'd finish at one restaurant and stagger to the next one in a sort of calorie-induced dementia. We laughed until we cried. Every time he told someone what we were doing, the story got more outrageous. At first, he said we had eaten at twenty restaurants in two days. Then it was thirty, then a hundred. He started calling our expedition the "Trail of Tears."

Of all the cities I wrote up for my article in *Texas Monthly*'s November 1999 issue, El Paso had the most on-target restaurant selections (except for my hometown, Austin), and I know who to thank. What other company head would cancel all his appointments for a day and also take a day of his weekend to help a reporter with a story that had nothing to do with his business? And take another day off when the reporter returned for a mop-up operation? Park did it because he cares deeply about El Paso and he wanted it to get some well-deserved recognition. Texas could use more men like this.

Sincerely,

Pat Sharpe

Patricia Sharpe
Senior Editor

MAYOR RON KIRK
HIS HONOR

TWICE ELECTED AS MAYOR OF THE GREAT CITY OF DALLAS!

My Texas post is: Mayor, City of Dallas, the best city in the country to work and play.

I came into this world on: June 27, 1954—with more hair than I have now.

I was born & raised in: Austin, TX, USA— where my mama led me down the political path.

I hang my hat in: The M streets in East Dallas.

I'm a real cowboy because: Roger Staubach told me so.

If you run into my friend Ann Richards ask her about: Our experiences on the campaign trail.

If you walked a mile in my boots: You'd probably be on the golf course.

I love Texas because: God blessed Texas!

"No one likes an insincere kiss-ass!"

— Mayor Ron's Favorite Texas Saying

SOUTHWEST AIRLINES CO.

Herbert D. Kelleher
Chairman of the Board,
President & Chief Executive Officer

P.O. Box 36611
Dallas, Texas 75235-1611
(214) 792-4110

Dear Martana:

When it comes to promoting Dallas, Ron Kirk is the Best Salesman In The World. I mean, he is the best marketeer since that famous fellow who sold those air conditioners to the Eskimos. How do I know: Well, let me tell you.

One day, these two impoverished entrepreneurs named Ross Perot, Jr. and Tom Hicks had an idea. It was a grand idea: the proverbial vision for a better Dallas. Their dream: build a huge expensive building in which millionaires could dribble a ball and swat a "puck." Their theory was that people like me (none of whom could possibly qualify for admission into Mensa) would pay large sums of money to observe such activities, usually while swilling mass quantities of liquid refreshment - which one can sympathize with. The problem was the usual one; impoverished entrepreneurs with a grand idea, but with insufficient assets. The solution: let the City of Dallas help build it. That's where Ron Kirk comes in.

Mayor Kirk, being a courageous and fearless leader, said, "Let the people decide." A vote was scheduled. The debate raged. Polls were taken. Consultants were hired. Democracy unfolded before our eyes. On the eve of the vote, fear ran rampant that the people might not see the grand vision. A brilliant strategy was conceived. It was this: get some unsuspecting schmuck who has no economic interest in this thing whatsoever to see the vision and pronounce it good. That's when Mayor Kirk called me. He said "Herb, it is a grand vision; it is good; pronounce it so - on T.V." Now, I'm here to tell ya that this man Ron Kirk is the King of all Salesmen. He told me the building would become famous; that anyone participating in the campaign would be forever blessed with perpetual prosperity and permanent good health; and that any corporation associated with it would never suffer from a falling stock price or endure investigation by the United States Securities and Exchange Commission, the World Court at the Hague, or even the Sheriff of Tarrant County. And, of course, I believed him. Because he is the Best Salesman In The World when it comes to promoting Dallas, Texas. That is how the Chairman of the Board, Chief Executive Officer and President of Southwest Airlines (that would be me) was persuaded to cut a T.V. commercial urging (successfully) people to vote for a new, huge, and expensive building now called - **THE AMERICAN AIRLINES ARENA.**

Like I said, when it comes to working on behalf of Dallas, Texas, Ron Kirk is the Best Salesman In The World. And, he is my friend. And, I love him. But, I still don't cotton to unpainted airplanes.

Best personal regards,

Herb

Herbert D. Kelleher

February 9, 2000

"Now, I'm here to tell ya that this man Ron Kirk is the King of all Salesmen."

I asked Herb Kelleher to write my "Tall Texas Tale" because: *Every word out of his mouth is a Tall Texas Tale.*

BOBBY LABONTE
NASCAR WINSTON CUP DRIVER

13 WINSTON CUP WINS!

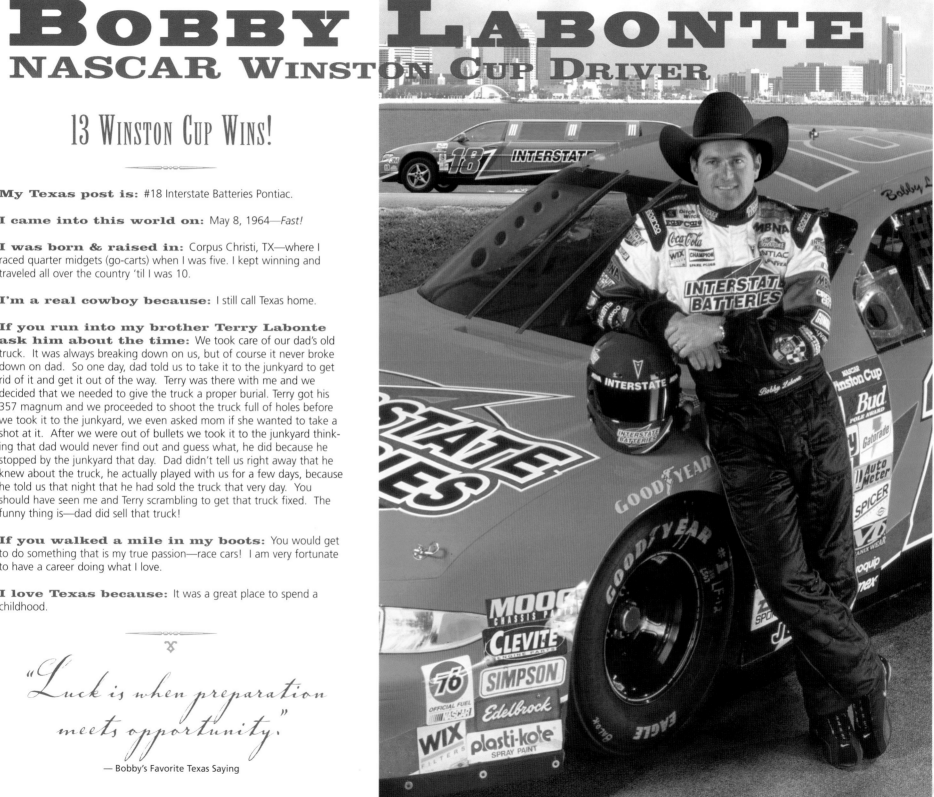

My Texas post is: #18 Interstate Batteries Pontiac.

I came into this world on: May 8, 1964—*Fast!*

I was born & raised in: Corpus Christi, TX—where I raced quarter midgets (go-carts) when I was five. I kept winning and traveled all over the country 'til I was 10.

I'm a real cowboy because: I still call Texas home.

If you run into my brother Terry Labonte ask him about the time: We took care of our dad's old truck. It was always breaking down on us, but of course it never broke down on dad. So one day, dad told us to take it to the junkyard to get rid of it and get it out of the way. Terry was there with me and we decided that we needed to give the truck a proper burial. Terry got his 357 magnum and we proceeded to shoot the truck full of holes before we took it to the junkyard, we even asked mom if she wanted to take a shot at it. After we were out of bullets we took it to the junkyard thinking that dad would never find out and guess what, he did because he stopped by the junkyard that day. Dad didn't tell us right away that he knew about the truck, he actually played with us for a few days, because he told us that night that he had sold the truck that very day. You should have seen me and Terry scrambling to get that truck fixed. The funny thing is—dad did sell that truck!

If you walked a mile in my boots: You would get to do something that is my true passion—race cars! I am very fortunate to have a career doing what I love.

I love Texas because: It was a great place to spend a childhood.

"Luck is when preparation meets opportunity."

— Bobby's Favorite Texas Saying

I asked Norm Miller to write my "Tall Texas Tale" because:

He's a great person and a great friend. Norm is the Chairman of Interstate Battery System of America, Inc., the primary sponsor of #18 car.

" . . . he still finds it hard to pass by a Whataburger without stopping."

June 15, 2000

It's a pleasure to write about this Lone Star son from Corpus Christi. Bobby Labonte's earliest memories are filled with his days racing go-karts on a dusty oval in his hometown. Now that he's one of the top four or so Winston Cup drivers, some of the same fans he had back then still cheer him on week after week. I think Texas loves him as much as he loves Texas.

I met Bobby back in 1994 when Joe Gibbs was considering him for his race team's new driver. Since Interstate Batteries is title sponsor of the team, Joe wanted me to see how I liked this "young buck." I liked him very much right away, and now that he wins so much, I have grown to love him dearly! Even though a lot of fame comes along with his success, Bobby can still get his head in his cowboy hat. He has learned to keep his cool, and he's downright funny, kind of a prankster when he's not running a race. Rare to find such a wonderful sense of humor on someone so focused on winning.

Early on Bobby and I found out that we share a love for fishing. Especially bass fishing on some good ol' Texas lakes. 'Course, it's not just the fishing. When you get Bobby out on the water, he's full of Texas-sized tales. And when it's something about his kids, he can talk a good, long while. I remember one story he told about his son Tyler...

Bobby had a chance to stay at home the night before a race at Charlotte Motor Speedway, a short drive from where he hangs his hat these days. (But he'll tell ya, his heart remains deep in the heart of Texas.) Probably about five at the time, Tyler had made his way to find Bobby and his wife Donna during the middle of the night and crawled into bed with them. At dawn Bobby was up and was creeping around the dark room getting ready to head to the track when he noticed Tyler sitting up in bed. If memory serves, the conversation went something like this:
"Daddy, is that you?" "Yeah, yeah, it's me Tyler." "Daddy? Are you racing today?" "Yeah Tyler. Go on back to sleep now. I'll see you there." "But Daddy, are you going to make some adjustments on the car today?" "Sure Tyler. We do every race." "Are you gonna talk a lot on the radio?" "Yeah Tyler. We will." "Good! That's what Jeff Gordon does when he wins." Just what Dad wanted to hear before a race. But wouldn't you know who won the Coca Cola 600 that day... Jeff Gordon!

Even though his race and appearance schedule is pretty overwhelming, Bobby makes a point to share his time with several charity organizations including The Cody Unser First Step Foundation, Winston Cup Wives Auxiliary, Motor Racing Outreach and many events that help children, such as the Make-A-Wish Foundation.

He is a wonderful role model. The kind of hero kids should have.

No doubt his Texas roots have something to do with the kind of man Bobby Labonte has grown to be. And I can tell he misses the little things... he still finds it hard to pass by a Whataburger without stopping. Guess that goes to show, you can take a Labonte out a Texas, but you can't take the Texas out of Labonte.

All the best,

Norm Miller
Chairman

12770 MERIT DRIVE · SUITE 400 · DALLAS, TEXAS 75251 · (972) 991-1444 · FAX (972) 458-8288 · www.interstatebatteries.com

JOE T. LANCARTE, SR.
JOE T. GARCIA'S TEX-MEX RESTAURANT

WON JAMES BEARD AWARD FOR BEST REGIONAL RESTAURANT

My Texas post is: Joe T. Garcia's Restaurant in Fort Worth, TX—around the corner from the stockyards.

I came into this world on: November 18, 1958, on a cool margarita night.

I was born & raised in: Fort Worth, TX, in a little kitchen on the north side of Fort Worth.

I hang my hat in: Fort Worth, TX.

I'm a real cowboy because: I love Texas and everything it stands for.

If you run into my friend Harvey ask him about the time we: Were hunting pheasant and I crawled over an electric fence. I don't remember much of what happened after I fell six feet and hit my head, but Harvey said I woke up thinking I was in the kitchen!

If you walked a mile in my boots: You would realize that I walk farther than a mile every day working in my family's restaurant.

I love Texas because: The people are real and Texans are proud of who they are.

"Every man loves what he is good at."

— Joe's Favorite Texas Saying

I asked Janine Turner to write my "Tall Texas Tale" because: *She loves "Joe-T" and she loves Garcias. Janine has been a great friend of mine and I think the world of her.*

"His reply was a gallant, 'Hand me the keys—I'll fix it.'"

Janine Turner

Dear Martana,

Texas is a great big state and it is rumored that everything in Texas is big. Well, this is true. And when it comes to big hearts, big smiles and great big Southern hospitality, I can only think of one person and that person is Joe T. Lancarte. Joe embodies all of the Texas qualities that represent a true Texan: charm, gusto, bravery and brains. Being a Fort Worth girl, I have had the pleasure of both knowing and admiring Joe through mutual friends and one other essential ingredient of Texas: Mexican food! I have traveled far and wide and always maintain that the best Mexican food "in the world" is at his family owned Joe T. Garcia's restaurant. Joe is the grandson of Joe T. Garcia who established the restaurant in 1935.

It is Joe T. Lancarte who stands as the pillar of Joe T.'s, both figuratively and literally. During the countless times that I have frequented his restaurant, Joe is always there exuding warmth and friendliness. I have often observed Joe as he strides across the floor, flawlessly entertaining all of his guests. This is quite a feat for Texans are a loud, gregarious, fun-lovin' bunch. If he was ever overwhelmed, one would never know it because his smile genuinely radiates.

During one visit with my six-year-old niece, Tiffany, I arrived with true Texas Showiness in my little red Corvette. I recklessly revved into the gravel parking lot and right over the parking log! Jammed, absolutely stuck-my car dangled in mid-air like a teeter-totter. During our lunch I casually mentioned this to Joe. His reply was a gallant, "Hand me the keys—I'll fix it". And he did! Within five minutes he returned successfully. The keys were clinking in his hand to the tune of "God Bless Texas". To this day, I don't know how he did it. However, at that very moment, he exhibited those essential Texas attributes: Charm, gusto, bravery and brains.

Joe T. Lancarte—my friend and my hero.

Fondly,

Janine Turner

Janine Turner

JAMES H. LEE
STOCK MARKET DYNAMO

CREATED A BUSINESS THAT EVERYONE SAID WOULD FAIL. BUSINESS IS BOOMING!

My Texas post is: Co-founder, Momentum Securities, LLC. We're the largest electronic trading firm in the country, providing direct connectivity to the securities markets for professional traders.

I came into this world on: June 8, 1966.

I was raised in: Houston, TX.

I hang my hat in: Houston, TX, home of the Wildcatter spirit, with my wife Amy.

I'm a real cowboy because: I work hard and play hard, and never turn my back on a friend.

If you run into my friend Todd Benson ask him about the time: He dared me to ice skate at the Galleria in Houston. A cowboy can do anything right? I got out on the ice about as gracefully as a newborn calf. After a few minutes I thought I had it licked when a couple of pretty Texas girls started whistling at me from the balcony. Grinning like a possum, I looked up to tip my hat and fell, tripping over my skates and slicing a gash in my leg. The pretty girls left, thus ending my skating career.

If you walked a mile in my boots: You'd never have time to be bored.

I love Texas because: It's the center of the universe, plain and simple. When Neil Armstrong phoned home where'd he call? Houston. Any questions?

"If you want a pure drink of water, go to the head of the stream."

— James' Favorite Texas Saying

RICK PERRY

LIEUTENANT GOVERNOR OF TEXAS • PRESIDENT OF THE SENATE

May 23, 2000

Dear Martana:

Jim Lee is an extraordinary Texan worthy of recognition as one of Texas' "Big Guns, Rising Stars and Cowboys".

I first met Jim in the summer of 1997 and was impressed by his enthusiasm and his commitment to a better Texas. Jim speaks with passion about ensuring educational opportunity for every Texas child. But more than just espousing ideas about educational opportunity, Jim has put his convictions to work.

By funding a Presidential Scholarship in the College of Business at the University of Texas at Austin, Jim has the distinction of being the youngest Texan to ever endow a scholarship in the business school. His generosity will pave the way for young men and women of future generations to not only dream big dreams, but be empowered with the tools to achieve those dreams.

Jim is a modern-day version of the "Texas Cowboy", charting new frontiers through the limitless opportunities available with advances in technology.

His love for Texas and the unique people of this state is surpassed only by his love for his wife Amy, his family and his friends.

I commend you for recognizing Jim as one of our state's unique shining stars. I couldn't have made a better choice myself.

Sincerely,

Rick Perry

Rick Perry
Lieutenant Governor

Not Printed or Mailed at State Expense • THE CAPITOL, AUSTIN, TEXAS 78711-2068 • 512 463 0001 • 800 441 0373 • TDD: 800 735 2989

" . . . Jim has the distinctiuon of being the youngest Texan to ever endow a scholarship in the business school."

I asked Rick Perry to write my "Tall Texas Tale" because:

If I weren't me, I'd want to be Rick. He's a true Texan in every sense of the word. He's not a "good time" friend, he's an "all the time" friend.

DOUG LEVY
CHIEF INTERNET WRANGLER

TexasMonthly.

Internet Web site: www.texasmonthly.com

P. O. Box 1569, Austin TX 78767-1569
Phone (512) 320-6900 **Direct** (512) 320-6906
Fax (512) 320-7350 **E-mail** mlevy@texasmonthly.emmis.com

Michael R. Levy
Founder and Publisher

May 1, 2000

Martana
Texas Men
Suite 100-140
25 Highland Park Village
Dallas, TX 75205

Dear Martana,

Faster than a 1K file traveling over a T1 line, able to exceed high expectations in a dot-com industry, our hero seems to have x-ray vision when it comes to spotting hot business trends.

When you meet Doug Levy, president and founder of imc², the first thing you notice is how young he is. At 28, he's already started three successful companies. The second thing you notice is how smart he is. It's more than just the diploma from the Wharton School of Business and his Phi Beta Kappa certificate that hang on his office wall. There's something compelling and cutting edge about Doug Levy.

Doug has been involved in groundbreaking enterprises for years. In college, he started a highly successful discount textbook business called Campus Text that competed head-to-head with the University of Pennsylvania bookstore. It takes a certain kind of moxie to park a truckload of books on the doorstep of a campus bookstore that has operated as a monopoly for more than a century. Needless to say, legal battles ensued, and Doug took his David and Goliath story to the university and local press where he won a public relations battle.

Through his experiences running Campus Text, Doug learned a lot about marketing to college students. During his college years, he'd also caught on to the potential of this new media – the Web – and intended to take full advantage of it. So it was natural that after graduation he returned to Dallas to start Internet University, an online information and resource tool designed to interest, inform and entertain college students. He helped clients like American Express and AT&T figure out how to capture the attention of students through online advertising and promotions. When Internet University caught the attention of ABC Sports and they asked Doug to develop a Web site for Monday Night Football, imc² was born.

Today – just four short years later – imc² is an industry-leading pioneer in Internet business solutions. Under Doug's leadership, imc² has won accolades not only for its design and technology achievements, but also for the company's enviable record of client satisfaction and assembled staff of top-ranked consumer and business-to-business Internet professionals. With an anticipated growth rate of 400 percent in 2000, imc² is an exciting, dynamic and powerful force in the Internet industry, leading Fortune 500 companies like Procter & Gamble, Eli Lilly and Company, General Mills, and Wyndham Hotels and Resorts to success on the information highway.

While Doug is way too modest to admit to being a superhero, he's definitely a super guy and a super entrepreneur. He's one young Texan who is destined to fly high.

Sincerely,

Michael R. Levy

I asked Mike Levy to write my "Tall Texas Tale" **because:** *He's a cowboy through and through, plus he's got a great last name!*

"Faster than a 1K file traveling over a T1 line . . . our hero seems to have x-ray vision . . ."

Recognized the Power of the Internet Early & Raised His Company from a Tiny Calf to the Head of the Herd

My Texas post is: President, imc2, where we lasso great ideas and turn them into successful online marketing solutions.

I came into this world on: May 29, 1971 . . . just a year before the Internet made its first public appearance and when the World Wide Web wasn't even a gleam in its daddy's eye.

I was born & raised in: Dallas, TX.

I hang my hat in: The new Texas ranch—the Uptown area of Dallas.

I'm a real cowboy because: I'm a fourth-generation Texan, born and bred.

If you run into my college buddies ask them about: The time we rustled business from the bookstore. It was just like opening up a gate of fenced-in cows, when I ran a multi-million dollar textbook company out of a dorm room.

If you walked a mile in my boots: You'd be accompanied by my beautiful wife Alyce and our black Labrador Buster.

I love Texas because: It's got enough space for big ideas to grow.

"There's only three things in the world worth being: first, best or different."

— Doug's Favorite Texas Saying

CARL LEWIS
OLYMPIAN OF THE CENTURY & ACTOR

9 GOLD MEDALS IN TRACK & FIELD IN FOUR OLYMPIADS!

My Texas post is: Dining in my restaurant, WBG (World Beat Grille) in Houston and in Los Angeles focusing on an acting career.

I came into this world on: July 1, 1961—feet first!

I hang my hat in: Houston, TX, where I still run around my neighborhood, and in the streets of L.A.

I'm a real cowboy because: I work hard to achieve my goals.

If you run into my friend Leroy Burrelle ask him about the time: A group of us went canoeing. Two of our buddies fell out of the canoe and when we tried to rescue them they almost drown all of us. We politely declined to let them back into the canoe and told them we'd be back to get them.

If you walked a mile in my boots: You'd be wearing Nikes.

My ultimate Texas date would be: A run with a beautiful woman listening to jazz on a shared Walkman.

I love Texas because: This is where I became a man.

"Never give up!"

— Carl,s Favorite Texas Saying

UNIVERSITY OF HOUSTON

Track & Field • 3100 Cullen • Houston, Texas 77204-6742
713/743-9465 • Fax: 713/743-9488

June 30, 2000

To have had the opportunity to coach the greatest Olympian of the century for 18 years was more than a distinct honor. It was a dream.

At the beginning in 1979 when Carl Lewis and I started this incredible journey, I had no idea where it would lead. Ten gold medals in four Olympiads later, I'm still amazed. I didn't know what he had in mind at the time but Carl, thinking like the Texan he has become, certainly did.

Frederick Carlton Lewis, a "Texas-transplant" who has become a larger-than-life figure on the world's sports stage, had the picture in his mind. His vision for himself and his sport (track & field) was so large and ahead of its time that I would say it certainly was as grand as the lone star.

Carl was only 17 when we met for the first time. I was the head track & field coach at the University of Houston and he was a prep star from New Jersey who was easily one of the most recruited high school athletes in the country. Even then, he seemed to have a certain maturity about him that most high school kids don't have until they are much older.

Shortly after he enrolled at Houston, Carl came into my office and explained his vision. Though unheard of and maybe even a little crazy back in 1979, it actually now is a realistic goal for track & field athletes to have.

Carl's vision was that his future financial success and security would be a result of what he did best—track & field. That's a normal enough personal vision for anyone, to play their best "career card," but for Carl there was more. He also wanted track and field to one-day be a major and even professional sport in this country.

Keep in mind that 20+ years ago the thought of making a living as a track & field competitor was revolutionary. Where athletes of other sports had opportunities to enter the professional ranks, the track & field athlete didn't have competitive options after college. Carl wanted to be a financial success and he also wanted the next generation of track & field stars to have a chance to follow their own dreams.

Where it was once a distant and (to many) unlikely vision, it is now a reality. Track & field athletes can now make a nice living in their sport because Carl Lewis helped make it so. He made track & field "cool" and something the public admired. People wanted to see the young, flashy Carl win Olympic gold in 1984 and they wanted to see the older, even-graying, Carl win gold in Atlanta in 1996. He did win both times, and in two other Olympics in between.

Today's track stars can trace their lucrative competitive opportunities back to when Carl simply wanted things to be better for his family and his sport. Also, his vision reached further than just the United States. Carl's international reputation has helped his track & field revolution circle the globe.

In retrospect my vision was a lot narrower. I was only thinking of the daily, weekly and monthly training regime, and the goals we would try to reach on a competitive level at different points of the upcoming season. Carl had the bigger picture in mind, and it turned out to be even bigger than his adopted state that he has called home for the last 20 + years.

Now that's a Texas hero—someone whose deeds were larger than life and with a genuine tale of how one vision changed the world.

All the best

Tom Tellez

Tom Tellez
Head Track & Field Coach (Ret.)
University of Houston

"Carl was only 17 when we met for the first time."

I asked Tom Tellez to write my "Tall Texas Tale" because: *He is one of the men most responsible for my success as an athlete. He coached me to four Olympics.*

JAY LOMBARDO
PREMIER CUSTOM CLOTHIER

"Jay took on a big challenge, making a beefy 330 pound offensive linemen look as sharp as a jocular politician."

I asked Tony Martinez of ESPN to write my "Tall Texas Tale"
because: *I learned a long time ago—if you need someone to do something, get the best, and Tony is one of the best journalists anywhere, not to mention a good friend.*

ESPN THE WORLDWIDE LEADER IN SPORTS

Dear Martana,

Thank God for Jay Lombardo!

Ever watch TV sports in the "good 'ol days"? Remember those handsome jocks on set with wide screen ties and Technicolor suits? Who can forget the mustard colored blazers Jim McKay wore at the Kentucky Derby? No wonder those horses looked so nervous darting down the home stretch- even colorblind 3 year-olds were runnin' scared looking at the ill-suited network TV crew!

But now times have changed. When my friend Jay Lombardo opened *Lombardo Custom Apparel* in 1990, he began the slow arduous, painstaking task of creating a high fashion dress code for the movers and shakers in pro sports and in North Texas upper echelon business circles. Jay took on a big challenge, making a beefy 330 pound offensive linemen look as sharp as a jocular politician. Judging by his amazing list of clientele, Jay has been hugely successful.

Take Craig James for example. When the former SMU running back retired from pro football he stepped into the world of television sports. Within a few short years he's sitting at the anchor desk on one of the biggest pre-game show on television, CBS Sports, *NFL Today*. Craig's "bull in the china closet" rushing style is contrasted by a subtle, smooth as silk delivery on set, punctuated by just the right line delivered with a panache' that can only be achieved by looking the part. Jay was instrumental in advising Craig to use a conservative, understated style to match his natural folksy delivery. The result is a look that never clutters a busy show.

On the other end of the spectrum is Michael Johnson, the 1996 Summer Olympic Games hero and world record holder in both the 200 and 400 meters. Michael can often be seen in Dallas' finest eateries and social events looking regal and above all…*fast*. Here again Jay has worked with Michael for years, lending his expertise to create a look that is flashy, tasteful and definitely *custom*. Michael Johnson may be the world's fastest human, but then everyone else seems to slow down just to check him out.

Best of all, Jay realizes that the clothes alone do not make the man. Over the years his company has sponsored so many philanthropic events and charities it is impossible to single out one. He truly believes that a man is not only remembered by how he looks but by what he gives back. It's the key to his success.

Today Jay and several business leaders are working to bring the Olympic Games to North Texas in 2012. With a rolodex that includes the likes of Dallas Cowboys quarterback Troy Aikman, Dallas Mayor Ron Kirk, FOX Sports legend Pat Summerall, and Texas Governor G.W. Bush, no wonder Jay is confident he can get the word out!

Now if Jay can do us all a favor and get Dale Hansen into his store. Remember high definition television is here. We need Jay's help!

Best regards,

Tony Martinez
ESPN *SportsCentury* **Producer**

ESPN Production, Inc.
1200 Post Road East
Westport, CT 06880
Tel: 203-291-7000
Fax: 203-291-7100

My Clothes Were on Two GQ Covers by My 30th Birthday!

My Texas post is: Founder of Lombardo Custom Apparel in the Metroplex, where we create images and wardrobes that make men look their very best.

I came into this world: June 15, 1963, in the middle of a severe electrical storm.

I was raised in: Richardson, TX.

I hang my hat in: My backyard, with family and friends.

I'm a real cowboy because: I always buck the system.

If you run into my fraternity brothers ask them about the time I: Did anything and I will swear it was a lie!

If you walked a mile in my boots: You probably would be coming in to buy a new pair of shoes.

I love Texas because: Where else but Texas can you wear boots with your tux!

"Underpromise, overdeliver and remember that people are just people— treat everyone the same—with respect (even if they're not from Texas)."

— Jay's Favorite Texas Saying

ROBERT LOWRIMORE
TEXAS LOTTERY WINNER

MULTI-MILLION DOLLAR LOTTERY WINNER!

My Texas post is: President, REL Aviation & Marine, Inc. and Arlington Jet Charter Company, Inc. We're the "jet" part in "jet-set."

I came into this world on: August 28—whirling around and I haven't stopped since!

I was born & raised in: Born in Dallas and raised in Arlington, TX—where we use to keep exotic animals in the backyard until our buffalo escaped and chased after a school boy's lunch pail!

I hang my hat in: Arlington, TX and at my ranch in Cleburne.

I'm a real cowboy because: I have 5 jets, 11 helicopters, 2 King Airs and a cow.

If you run into my friend John Faltynski ask him about the time we: Flew Santa and his elves around for 40 hours, so he could visit children's hospitals around the Dallas/Ft. Worth metroplex. It was for SANTA USA, one of my favorite charities.

If you walked a mile in my boots: You'd believe in God and Quick Pick.

My ultimate Texas date would be: To hop on my private jet at sunset and fly to Key West. We'd drink a Crown & Seven with grilled Mahi Mahi, then cruise on my yacht to some remote island in the Bahamas.

I love Texas because: Winning the Texas lottery allowed me to share my fortune with my family, friends and local charities such as "Wish for Wings"—a program that donates free flights to terminally ill kids. Plus, the women in Texas ain't all bad either!

"You must have bumped your head."

— Robert's Favorite Texas Saying

J. GARY TRICHTER & ASSOCIATES
THE KIRBY MANSION
2000 SMITH STREET
HOUSTON, TEXAS 77002
TEL: (713) 524-1010
FAX: (713) 524-1080
www.texasdwilaw.com

CHRISTIAN C. SAMUELSON
Chris83072@aol.com
JASON D. CASSEL
jdcassel@flash.net
DOUG MURPHY
doug@murphyslaws.com

J. GARY TRICHTER
trixtr@netropolis.net
Licensed in Alaska
Colorado and Texas

June 28, 2000

Dear Martana:

I met Robert several years ago at Houston's Hobby Airport when I was but a fledging student helicopter pilot. I instantly liked him. Not only did he have a kind of "Jimmy Stewart" quiet innocence about him, but also he had a "Sam Elliott" country drawl to go with it. It didn't hurt that he was a very skilled and professional helicopter pilot, too!

As timed passed, Robert and I spent more time together and I soon learned that my first impression of him had not changed. Indeed, I came to believe and still do that when Robert won the Lottery, so did his family, friends and community. Without a doubt, he is one of the most warm and giving people I have ever met. He is quick to share both his money and himself with the needy, especially children and the elderly.

Being modest, Robert is not apt to brag on his good deeds, but I can and I'm honored to do so. During the past several years at Christmas time, Robert has personally given terminally ill children helicopter sightseeing trips over the Dallas-Fort Worth metroplex area. He also routinely flies Santa and his elves to elementary schools and nursing homes to share the Christmas Spirit. Of course, Robert does it all at his own expense. He logged over 100 volunteer flight hours last December.

Robert does not always work at his charter aviation business and when he vacations he knows how to have the type of fun people spin yarns about. One such trip took him on a scuba diving adventure to Fort Jefferson in the Dry Tortugas Islands off Key West. It was there that Robert, in search of giant conch shells, discovered the only known stealth barracuda with the "biggest set of teeth in the Gulf." It was then that the Navy received an unconfirmed report of a phantom torpedo surfacing at record speed with a bathing suit on. Legend then continues that Robert shot upward and cleared the boat rail without touching it. The barracuda remains stealth to this day because no one else credible saw it. The Navy's phantom torpedo investigation still remains open.

Most tall tales have a beginning, middle and an end, but not this one because Robert will continue sharing his "It's a Wonderful Life" existence with those who need it. You'll hear more about this Texan in the future and that's for sure.

His friend and proud of it,

J. Gary Trichter

J. Gary Trichter

OF COUNSEL

PAT WILLIAMS
HOUSTON, TEXAS
(713) 651-9883

JOHN C. BOSTON
AUSTIN, TEXAS
(512) 899-9425

BENNIE E. RAY
AUSTIN, TEXAS
(512) 479-7775

MIKE McCOLLUM
DALLAS, TEXAS
(214) 691-3975

" ... Robert ... discovered the only known stealth barracuda with the 'biggest set of teeth in the Gulf.'"

I asked Gary Trichter to write my "Tall Texas Tale" because: *We were in the Confederate Air Force together. He flys old exotic planes and I fly the helicopters. We're the guys you see looping around the sky.*

CARTER MALOUF
24 KARAT COWBOY

I asked Bob Schlegel to write my "Tall Texas Tale" because: *He and his whole family are not only loyal customers, but also epitomize Texas hospitality. I am honored to have them as clients and treasure their friendship.*

> "He was covered up in what looked like a man-eating flower arrangement, as only his legs were visible!"

Pavestone Company
4835 LBJ Freeway
Suite 700
Dallas, Texas 75244
972/404-0400
Fax 972/404-9200
www.pavestone.com

February 1, 2000

Dear Martana,

It was the day of my daughter, Kimberly's *debutante ball.* The event was taking place at our home in Dallas. The tents were erected and the flowers were being put in place when in walks, Carter Malouf. Carter had told my wife, Myrna and Kim that he wished, for her day as the 'princess of Dallas', to be adorned with the appropriate jewelry. I did not know exactly what he meant until later when, to my surprise and amazement, the crown jewels appeared strewn around my wife's neck and ears, along with Kim, and my two other daughters, Kari and Krystal. Needless to say, I was *spellbound* when I saw them, knowing my insurance man would certainly ask me at the party if they had been scheduled! **As a typical father of the debutante, I wanted everything to be perfect.** I wanted Kim to know the happiest night of her life and seeing her in some of the spectacular pieces Carter brought, I realized that my little girl has grown up and the description of "princess" was well understated.

After dropping off the jewels to the house, Carter returned a second time. He was covered up in what looked like a man-eating flower arrangement, as only his legs were visible! As I later learned, Carter has put this entire arrangement together in our parking area, and it barely fit through the door. "Sorry to interrupt," Carter began, "I just had to give you something before the evening progresses. You all have been very good to me. You have put your faith in me and entrusted me to help you and your family. Not only that, you have provided me with excellent referrals for my business. I just wanted to use this special evening to return the favor." Needless to say, with all the planning this event had seen, there was some controversy as to where this five-foot tall bouquet should be placed. As fortune would have it, the library turned out to be the perfect venue for such an awesome display of flowers.

All I can say is that I have it on my list to thank Carter about five million times! He helped make the most important night of my daughter's life that much more special. Thanks, Carter for everything!

By the way, do we really have to return the jewelry?

Sincerely,

Robert J. Schlegel
Chairman

ANCHOR WALL SYSTEMS   World Wide UNI Pavers   SYMETRY PAVING SYSTEMS

Dallas/Fort Worth • Austin/San Antonio • Chattanooga • Cincinnati • Denver • Houston • Kansas City • Las Vegas • New Orleans • Phoenix • St. Louis

Best Chef of the Malouf Family!
My Specialty: Spanish Beef with Cascabell-Chili-Aioli Sauce

My Texas post is: Expert in estate and fine jewelry for William Noble Jewelers located right on Charles Goodnight's historic Texas cattle trail in Highland Park Village.

I came into this world on: January 19, 1966 . . . it was a dazzling day.

I was born & raised in: "Big D"— I always thought it stood for "Big Diamonds."

I hang my hat in: Dallas, but I keep ball caps in Santa Fe and McKinney, TX.

I'm a real cowboy because: I have a Labrador retriever and alligator boots!

If you run into my friend Bill Noble ask him about: Jim Green from Abilene. If you can get through the rest of his jokes, then maybe you'll make it through to the one he always tells—about me being like Jim Green from Abilene.

If you walked a mile in my boots: You'd wonder why women always want to touch your head.

My ultimate Texas date would be: Over a dinner of Spanish beef, cooked by me and served on the top floor of The Mansion suite while two flamenco guitarists play music by the Gypsy Kings.

I love Texas because: Of its beautiful land—The Big Bend area, the Southwest, Texas Hill Country, East Texas, the Coast and . . . certain aspects of West Texas.

"Those who never get carried away should be."

— Carter's Favorite Texas Saying

L. WILLIAM McNUTT, JR.
THE WORLD'S ORIGINAL FRUITCAKE BAKER

COLLIN STREET BAKERY SELLS FRUITCAKES TO EVERY COUNTRY IN THE WORLD EXCEPT TWO —103 YEARS & COUNTING!

My Texas post is: Collin Street Bakery.

I came into this world on: June 16, 1925, with a sweet tooth.

I was born & raised in: Corsicana, where the first Texas oil well was ever drilled.

I hang my hat in: Corsicana, TX—home of the Fighting Tigers.

I'm a real cowboy because: Native Texans are supposed to be.

If you run into my friend John Crawford ask him about the time: We took "showgirls" to Las Vegas. John, myself and our wives were driving to Las Vegas and stopped on the way at a little roadside filling station. Our good-looking wives, wearing the capri pants that were stylish then, got out of the car to freshen up. The gas attendant glanced at our wives and then leaned over and whispered to us, "Are those showgirls?" This is a story we still laugh about today.

If you walked a mile in my boots: You'd be tired because we deliver one and a half million fruitcakes during the holidays.

"Everyday I try to sell fruitcakes—not be one."

— Bill's Favorite Texas Saying

KANSAS CITY CHIEFS

One Arrowhead Drive • Kansas City, Missouri 64129 • (816) 924-9300 • FAX 816-922-4296

LAMAR HUNT
Founder

Reply to:
1601 Elm Street
Suite 4000
Dallas, TX 75201
(214) 720-1601
FAX (214) 720-1617

October 19, 1999

Dear Martana,

This year is the 40th Anniversary of the start of the American Football League, and it reminds me that on July 30 of 1959, I went to get on a commercial flight out to the Bay area and ran into an acquaintance - Bill McNutt of Collin Street Bakery fame - a real Texas business "original". I had run into Bill previously at several college football games, and on this occasion I asked him why he was going to San Francisco. His answer was straight to the point, "I'm going to see your football team - the Dallas Texans", who were scheduled to play their very first game in their history against the Oakland Raiders the next day at Kezar Stadium in San Francisco - a preseason game, no less!

Well, we all probably know that:

a)   Bill was serious, in that he did indeed go to the Texans-Raiders game.

b)   Bill, as much as anything, was going to San Francisco to help sell Collin
        Street Bakery fruitcakes and find himself a good steak dinner.

Through the years, I would estimate that I have probably attended 300 plus sporting events with Bill McNutt. These run the full gamut - from World Cup soccer matches in Spain, Mexico, Germany, Italy and the United States, to countless other pro sporting events, including about 30 Super Bowls, as well as other pro, college and high school football and basketball games, pro tennis matches, the Olympics, Major League baseball games and a horse race or two, etc. I'm sure if I thought about it, I could come up with a "marbles" face off or a "hopscotch" championship along the line too.

His game is "Fruitcakes", and he is the best in the world, but he isn't too bad at "sports", as well.

Sincerely,

Lamar Hunt
LH:sn

Charter Member, American Football Conference, National Football League

I asked Lamar Hunt to write my "Tall Texas Tale" because: *I knew he would lie for me!*

" . . . I have probably attended 300 plus sporting events with Bill McNutt."

WYMAN MEINZER
THE EYE OF TEXAS

OFFICIAL STATE PHOTOGRAPHER OF TEXAS BY APPOINTMENT OF THE 75TH LEGISLATURE & GOVERNOR GEORGE W. BUSH

My Texas post is: Drifting the High Plains with my camera and shooting over $10,000 in film per year.

I came into this world on: November 4, 1950, with a desire for adventure—that adventure defines my life.

I was born & raised in: Born in Benjamin, TX and raised nearby on a 27,000 acre ranch on the Brazos River where my dad was a foreman.

I hang my hat in: The 1887 historical jailhouse in Benjamin. My bedroom is the old cellblock and my office is the old sheriff's office!

I'm a real cowboy because: I love the adventure and excitement in everyday life. If I can't have fun working—then I don't want to work. I always have so much damn fun!

If you run into my friend Knut Mjolhus ask him about the time we: Were in a helicopter flying over the Rio Grande River shooting for a book project. I kept screaming at the clouds to move out of my way . . . the clouds suddenly parted and the light ignited the canyon. It took our breath away.

If you walked a mile in my boots: I think you would possess a love and affection for Texas previously thought unattainable.

My ultimate Texas date would be: In far West Texas—photographing thunderstorms from a helicopter.

I love Texas because: Of its big skies and pioneer spirit exhibited by so many people in the plains and West Texas.

"Bull %#¢!"*

— Wyman's Favorite Texas Saying

RAY SASSER
2136 CHISHOLM TRAIL   ROCKWALL, TEXAS 75087   (214) 722-1933

Dear readers:

Riding through the Texas badlands with Wyman Meinzer feels like sharing a crewcab pickup with Vincent Van Gogh, Kit Carson, James Michener and John Muir—all at the same time and all vying for attention.

We're bouncing along a rough, rutted ranch road when the Kit Carson-Wyman points out the cabin—shack really—where he spent bitter winters running a trapline for coyotes. That mountain man persona is amplified by Wyman's choice of knee-high, snakeproof boots, jeans and wool shirts as standard wardrobe. When Wyman spoke to Texas Tech University's summer commencement in 1999, he had to buy a suit for the occasion.

We lurch over a massive hill and Wyman points out where a pioneer expedition came through the region in the 1800s. Nobody knows the route for sure, but Wyman has figured it out based on landmarks noted in the expedition log. He's a more precise historian than James Michener and often gives lectures at the Knox County courthouse a literal stone's throw from his home. That home, incidentally, is a 100-year-old jail that Wyman converted to a unique and comfortable abode.

Though we haven't seen another human being for three hours, Wyman quickly shifts to his John Muir, naturalist/protectionist mode. He decries the damage done by a growing Texas population to this land he so fiercely loves. Then he slams on his brakes, snatches the ever-present camera from behind the seat and leaps out to capture a fleeting photo opportunity of flowering cactus that few people—including an artist like Vincent Van Gogh—would have noticed. That's the Wyman Meinzer that most people think they know—the photographer who sees indescribable beauty in a bleak landscape, then describes the beauty with vivid photographs. The Wyman Meinzer I know is a complex personality in a simple shell. In more ways than one, he is a straight shooter.

Sincerely,

Ray Sasser

Ray Sasser

"Riding through the Texas badlands with Wyman Meinzer feels like sharing a crewcab pickup with Vincent Van Gogh . . . "

I asked Ray Sasser to write my "Tall Texas Tale" because: *Ray appreciates the passion I have for the Texas experience.*

GUY MEZGER
WORLD KICKBOXING CHAMPION

THREE-TIME KING OF PANCRASE
[WORLD TITLE IN "FREE-FIGHTING"]
& ULTIMATE FIGHTING CHAMPION

My Texas post is: Owner of Guy Mezger's Freestyle Training Centers in Dallas, TX, where I teach fitness and martial arts to adults and children, when I am not duking it out in some competition.

I came into this world on: January 1, 1968 (I just missed being a New Year's baby by 1 hour & 13 minutes!).

I was born & raised in: Born in Houston, TX & raised in and around the Dallas area.

I hang my hat in: Dallas, TX—lower Greenville Avenue.

I'm a real cowboy because: I was born in Texas; I learned how to ride horses by age 10; love a good steak; & will always be a gentleman (something all real Texas men are).

If you run into my plastic surgeon ask him: How many times he has had to fix my nose—13 broken noses and counting!

If you walked a mile in my boots: You would be tired—my day is long & hard . . . even painful if you consider what I do for a living.

I love Texas because: Texas is an original from the land to the people. It is definitely cool to be from Texas!

"The harder I train, the luckier I get."

— Guy's Favorite Texas Saying

> " . . . despite having had his nose broken 12 times is still able to maintain his Hollywood good looks. "

I asked Master Ron Van Browning to write my "Tall Texas Tale" because: *He has known me for quite a while and has seen me grow to be the person that I am today. As a fellow Martial Artist and a former professional fighter, he understands the unusual code which we live by.*

TRAINERS ELITE
The Ultimate In Self Protection

June 6, 1998

Dear Martana,

In your search for true <u>Texas Men</u>, you need look no further than the martial arts arena. Here is a sport that requires physical ability, discipline, determination, focus and drive. In a sport that can sometimes be extremely brutal and where egos are always larger than life, you find a man who encompasses all these things – His Royal Highness, Guy Mezger.

Why the title HRH you ask? Guy has had 136 full contact fights, from karate and kickboxing, to freestyle fighting. Guy has held 4 world titles in 4 contact sports, including King of Pancrase, the ultimate title in a hybrid sport in Japan that incorporates kickboxing and Greco-Roman wrestling. In a sport where fighters look as tough and mean as the streets they come from, here is a man who despite having had his nose broken 12 times is still able to maintain his Hollywood good looks. (He's still waiting for Hollywood to call).

Guy has fought the best fighters in the world and two things stand out: first, he won; second, and more importantly, he always fought by the rules – no cheap shots, which is almost unheard of in professional fighting. To most competitors, Guy is seen as a bad man, but he has never wanted to hurt someone just to win, which makes him a true sportsman.

There is one weakness for this true Texas man: children. Training kids is his passion. They are an important part of his life and he will be the first to tell you they help keep his feet firmly on the ground. Guy is a real Texas man, and to prove it, look no further than in the eyes of the kids who look up to him.

Sincerely,

Master Ron Van Browning

17370 Preston Road
Suite 450
Dallas, Texas 75252
214/931-0867

AL MICALLEF
TEXAS CATTLE BARON

MANAGES RANCHING OPERATIONS ON OVER 150,000 ACRES & RUNS 10,000 HEAD OF CATTLE A YEAR

My Texas post is: The C.F. Ranch in Alpine, TX, Jaritas Ranch in New Mexico, and our headquarters, JMK International, Fort Worth, TX.

I came into this world on: January 6, 1943, but in spirit I've been here forever.

I hang my hat in: Alpine, TX.

I'm a real cowboy because: I'm not a real cowboy. I'm a rancher, but I respect the boys that are real cowboys.

If you run into my friend Brad Johnson ask him about the time I: Roped a turkey. It's really hard to un-rope a turkey. We ended up having to let it go— rope and all!

If you walked a mile in my boots: You'd still be lost, because I wouldn't stop to ask for directions!

I love Texas because: It's brash and beautiful.

"If you're not making dust, you're eating dust."

— Al's Favorite Texas Saying

Brad Johnson

Dear Martana,

Al called me one day and said, "Brad, I want to go to the National Finals Rodeo in Las Vegas, can you help me?" I said, "Sure, I can find you some tickets." Al said, "No, I want to go to the National Finals, I want to compete there in the team roping." Not only had this fifty-year-old man never roped, he was left handed to boot! Needless to say, the odds were stacked against him. Undaunted, he got to work.

The tenacity and determination I witnessed during the few months that followed, I've yet to see equaled. Although Al hasn't made the National Finals Rodeo, (yet) he can hold his own with the best in the world (right handed no-less). But anyone who knows this man has seen this same scenario played out time and time again.

Whether it's ranching, flying, restaurants, book publishing or finding new innovative ideas to better his community, just don't tell Al Micallef it can't be done, because the words are not in his vocabulary.

Sincerely,

Brad Johnson

7920 Sunset Blvd., Ste. 401, Los Angeles, CA 90046 (213) 969-0700
9830 Wilshire Blvd., Beverly Hills, CA 90212-1825 (310) 288-4545

"Not only had this fifty-year-old man never roped, he was left handed to boot!"

I asked Brad Johnson to write my "Tall Texas Tale" because: *He's my only friend who can write.*

MIKE MULLEN
MILLIONAIRE TEXAS BACHELOR

ABC Radio Networks

Dear Martana,

The history of real Texas men perhaps begins with Sam Houston, Davy Crockett, and Jim Bowie. None of them were born in the state that would be great, but they certainly set the standard for the native-born or "naturalized" Texans to follow. From the legendary Texas rancher and gunfighter Clay Allison to Frank "Bring-em-back-alive" Buck, to oilman H.L. Hunt, to Gail Borden Jr. of milk fame, to trailsman Charles Goodnight to Ross Perot, men who call Texas home are an aggressive, glamorous, entrepreneurial, innovative, tenacious, far-sighted bunch. They become legends in their own time and in our minds. That's why Mike Mullen is my choice for a real Texas man.

This Dallas native son has certainly seen more than his allotted fifteen minutes of fame. His time in the spotlight began in 1998 thanks to the "most eligible bachelor" status conferred on him by "Oprah"; "Inside Edition"; Spanish, German and Australian television; Marie Claire magazine and Woman's Day magazine. Beyond all of the headlines and media glare, however, is the real Mike Mullen. And he is a Texas man indeed. Using foresight and the savvy gained working in the oil fields of Iran and the North Sea, Mike used carefully accumulated funds to purchase drilling rigs during the crash of 1982. Like many an astute millionaire before him, he saw an opportunity, risked all and took it. In the process, he made himself a fortune. Now he uses that monetary reward for his efforts to further his business ventures, fund a certain lifestyle (four homes, a helicopter, a jet and a yacht), assure the futures of his 17-year-old-daughter and 8-year-old twin boys, and contribute unselfishly to a multitude of local charities.

This one–time Tulane University football star is remarkably fit due to a rigorous workout schedule and prudent habits (healthy foods, no drinking, no drugs, no smoking). His quick wit, clever mind, and dancing brown eyes are all a testament to the power of clearheaded perception and clean-living. Handsome, sophisticated yet down-to-earth, Mike may not be searching for a bride, but would-be-brides are searching for him. After all, aren't extraordinary Texas knights on white horses few and far between?

Fondly,

Jocelyn W

Jocelyn White

13725 Montfort Drive Dallas, TX 75240-4452 (972) 991-9200

abc

I asked Jocelyn White to write my "Tall Texas Tale" because: *I have known Jocelyn for many years and have admired her talents in radio and TV, as well as her charitable contribution to community. I am honored that she has written my "Tall Texas Tale."*

" . . . Mike may not be searching for a bride, but would-be-brides are searching for him."

1999 Hatteras-Bertram Shootout & Poco Bueno Blue Marlin Tournament Champion (600 lb. Blue Marlin)

My Texas post is: President, Energy Equipment Resources in Dallas, TX.

I came into this world on: February 4, 1950 in shining armor.

I was born & raised in: Dallas, TX.

I hang my hat in: Paluxy, TX at the 4M Ranch; Rockport, TX at the Bali house; Snowmass Village, CO at a mountain hideaway; and Dallas, TX at my Meadowbrook estate.

I'm a real cowboy because: I am not afraid to try anything.

If you run into my friend Oprah ask her about the time I: Was featured on her Oprah Texas show in the winter of `98 where she tried on a 14-carat diamond ring that I am saving for my future wife. I received over 60,000 letters after that appearance!

If you walked a mile in my boots: You would be recognized by many people.

My ultimate Texas date would be: Fighting a 600 lb. blue marlin with one arm while holding the woman of my dreams in the other.

I love Texas because: It is wide open and anything goes!

"Don't ask a Texan if it can be done, because he will tell you he has already done it."

— Mike's Favorite Texas Saying

SCOTT MURRAY
SPORTS ANCHOR & EMCEE EXTRAORDINAIRE

"He's been known to emcee two events simultaneously."

I asked Helen Bryant to write my "Tall Texas Tale" because: *She always has the latest gossip in her newspaper column on anybody, to anything, from anyplace so how could I go wrong allowing someone with such impeccable taste, incredible connections and unmatched knowledge to perform such a task? As my kids would say, "That's a no brainer Dad." (Gosh, now I sound like a male version of Helen herself.)*

The Dallas Morning News

Dear Martana:

It's just impossible to go anywhere in Dallas–Fort Worth area without running into Scott Murray.

Scott emcees more benefits, rides in more parades and makes more celebrity charity appearances than any other media person in the Dallas – heck. probably more than anybody in any market in the world. And somehow, he still finds time to show up at Channel 5. He's been known to emcee two events simultaneously. (It works if they're in the same hotel).

Scott can introduce a roomful of special guests in 60 seconds flat. He can fill embarrassing gaps in programs. He can even sing! He handled a solo in the 1999 Dallas Press Club Gridiron Show beautifully (but he's not quitting his day job). And his wife, Carol, is always there at his side. Lord knows she's had her fill of hotel chicken by now.

One of my favorite Scott Murray moments: In 1993, he was playing a game of Celebrity Monopoly at the Anatole to benefit Love for Kids. That was the day we all saw the real Scott Murray.

He eagerly erected one hotel complex after another all over the board. He won the game – then headed off to the next event he had to emcee.

Helen Bryant

Communications Center, P.O. Box 655237, Dallas, Texas 75265, 214/977-8222

My Texas post is: The Dallas Fort Worth Metroplex—"The greatest sports community in the country with the most benevolent people in the world."

I came into this world on: A Sunday . . . just in time for kickoff.

I was born & raised in: The bottom of the ninth, bases loaded, two outs, and a 3-2 count.

I hang my hat in: Arenas, stadiums and ballparks, all across America.

I'm a real cowboy because: "I know when to hold 'em and I know when to fold 'em. "

If you run into my friend actress Janine Turner ask her about the time: She sent a limo for me to join her for the opening night debut of her movie *Leave it to Beaver*. The limo got caught in traffic, so I had to get out and walk in my tuxedo with my wife in her formal for about ten blocks. Finally, as we were less than a block away from the theatre, the limo pulled up alongside of us after getting through traffic! We hopped back in and arrived just in time . . . like nothing had ever happened. (Wonder if Eddie Haskel had anything to do with our misfortune?)

If you walked a mile in my boots: You'd have accumulated more speedway oil, football turf, diamond dirt and sports tales than you could share in a lifetime.

I love Texas because: I can roam and roam, be in a zone, and still call it home.

"Live each day with a helping hand, a motivated mind and a courageous heart."

— Scott's Favorite Texas Saying

STEVE MURRIN
TEXAS WESTERN CULTURE PRESERVATIONIST

415 Throckmorton
Fort Worth, Texas 76102 ★ USA
817/336-8791 ★ 800/433-5747
FAX 817/336-3282
www.fortworth.com

Convention & Visitors Bureau

January 7, 1998

Dear Martana:

Texas men have long had the reputation for being something special. This image goes back to the early days of the Lone Star State when it took courage to open up this "wild and wooly" land for ranching and towns. Adventuresome characters gave Texas its beginning from the frontier years of trail drives, boom and bust oil days, extraordinary weather calamities and on to international business and the conquest of space. Steve Murrin of Fort Worth exemplifies this special character which has made Texas great over the years.

There are probably few persons that look more Texan than Steve Murrin with his bushy mustache, big cowboy hat, ever present bandana and tall boots. The lanky Murrin, with his distinctive Texas drawl, looks like he just left the trail drive, ready to "wet his whistle" at Billy Bob's Texas or the White Elephant Saloon. But Murrin does not just look Texan; he is thoroughly Texan, with unique Lone Star credentials to match anyone in this big state.

The Murrins first came to Fort Worth in the 1880s when Steve's grandfather had a saloon on Front Street, across from the train depot, another across from the Courthouse and a third on Main, between the others. His father worked as a cowboy in the Stockyards, had a well-known restaurant on Camp Bowie, and later a ranch on the west side of Fort Worth. His mother came to the city from Mexico during the Revolution, and as a result, Steve is fluent in Spanish. Steve went to Arlington Heights High School, Holy Cross and U.T. Austin. After college, he went into real estate where his devotion to revitalization of the historic Stockyards developed. He saw the Armour and Swift plants closed down and knew that this historic treasure might be lost to the city and the state unless new uses for the Stockyards could be found.

Steve Murrin became a leader in the early uphill fight to preserve the historic Stockyards as a cultural tourism gem of the State of Texas. Many local people did not share his keen love of the Stockyards traditions and history, and the last 25 years has taken a tremendous effort by Steve Murrin and others to ensure that the historic buildings and authentic atmosphere of the Stockyards could become a great visitor experience for people of the state and from throughout the country and world. As a result of his many contributions to making the Stockyards and traditional Texas culture a major tourism industry, Steve Murrin received the prestigious 1996 Charles Goodnight Award. This is one of the top honors given to persons who have contributed significantly to Texas ranch and western culture. Steve Murrin epitomizes Texas western culture from head to toe and is a major factor in the growth of tourism in the Lone Star State.

Sincerely yours,

Doug Harman

Douglas Harman
President & CEO

> "The lanky Murrin, with his distinctive Texas drawl, looks like he just left the trail drive . . ."

I asked Doug Harman to write my "Tall Texas Tale" because: *Well, he came here from Virginia, a state that appreciates heritage . . . he recognizes and appreciates the positive potential of Fort Worth's ranch, cattleman, cowboy, stockyard, packing-house history and how it fits as a foundation for the city's future, both aesthetically and economically.*

RESTORED HISTORIC FORT WORTH STOCKYARDS & RECEIVED CHARLES GOODNIGHT AWARD

My Texas post is: I feel pretty comfortable just about anywhere West of Highway 360 (Dallas County Line).

I came into this world on: July 1, 1938—with my hat on.

I was born & raised in: Fort Worth, TX.

I hang my hat at: The family ranch, the Westfork, west of Fort Worth.

If you run into my friend Dallas Mayor Ron Kirk ask him about the time: Me and my partner Jimbo Calhoun rode horses over to Dallas City Hall to deliver an invitation from our city council for the mayor to come over and visit Fort Worth occasionally to get a little relief from the mosquitoes and Yankees that hang around in Dallas . . . tell him the invitation still stands.

I'm a real cowboy because: I've known and worked with some real cowboys from time to time while I was growing up, so I don't claim to be a real cowboy. I couldn't tote most of them's rope, but I've always enjoyed being around them—just trying to be a little bit of help and not get in the way.

If you walked a mile in my boots: You'd have sore feet, boots are meant for ridin'—not walkin'.

I love Texas because: Texans are presumed to be friendly, honest and strong in their convictions, which are generally thought to be solid.

"Fort Worth is West Texas, and Dallas is East Coast."

— Steve's Favorite Texas Saying

TOM NALL
THE "CHILI MAN"

MAKING THE GUINESS BOOK OF RECORDS FOR TORTILLA EATING: 74 IN 30 MINUTES & DEVELOPING WICK FOWLER'S 2-ALARM CHILI KITS!

My Texas post is: Austin, TX—where I've been involved with 2-Alarm Chili for well over 25 years and have seen it grow from a hobby to a successful food company. My roles have been marketing, sales and spokesperson, but I've swept the floors, unloaded trucks and worked in production; all the necessary jobs.

I came into this world on: The 23rd of February 1943, and my Momma won't like me sayin' I was born that long ago.

I was born & raised in: Garland, TX—a big city that was once a little country town.

I hang my hat in: A wonderful log home deep in the Texas Hill Country between Marble Falls and Burnet, TX.

I'm a real cowboy because: My dad taught me what real cowboy life is about—hard work, which isn't very glamorous unless you're horseback.

If you run into my friend Jim Tugmon, alias "Bob Wire," ask him about the time: We had finished a cattle drive on Quinlan Ranch in southern Colorado and "cut a trail" to Sante Fe, NM where we were asked to leave a popular saloon twice in one night. Well, that was just the "cowboy way."

If you walked a mile in my boots: You could be in Texas, Colorado, New Mexico, Oklahoma or Arizona on any given day!

I love Texas because: We've got so much to brag about—from the mountains of Big Bend to the beaches of the Gulf Coast, big timber in East Texas, ranch and farm land in West Texas, and wonderful towns like Luckenbach, Terlingua, Dime Box, Zephyr, Lajitas, Rockne, Sisterdale, Turkey . . . no one talks about their state the way Texans do.

"Any weather is chili weather."

—Tom's Favorite Texas Saying

Sometime in the year 2000

Dear Martana,

Fifteen years ago I met Tom Nall at a fancy food show, where I spent considerable time trying to convince him that he needed to be mixing RED EYE BLOODY MARY MIX with his TWO-ALARM CHILI MIX. Likewise he tried to convince me TWO-ALARM didn't need a dadgum thing and that I belonged on a cattledrive. He was right about both accounts. Both of us born about 100 years too late, we became fast friends. Tom is a man of honor who works hard and plays hard. Sometimes, much to the surprise of others.

Not so very long ago, Tom and his legendary brother, Blue, met up with Gordon Fowler and Rod Patrick over in Lockhart just after Rod brought his 18 month old prize bull along on it's way through our capital city. As fate would have it, these men had been "overserved" at that famous BBQ joint there in Lockhart and decided that the advertising agency Tom was dealing with had never been properly introduced to one of the main ingredients in TWO-ALARM CHILI. Now, this bull was gentle, agreed, but could he be that gentle? A bet ensued. They drove to Austin.

Somewhere down on Sixth Street, upstairs, the unsuspecting ad firm of Moore & More was greeted by an immediate entrance. Having had his body pierced with a nose ring, the bull would follow a lead rope just about anywhere. And it did. Up 24 straight stairs and a sharp right turn directly into the lobby of the advertising agency. Now Tom has always been able to turn heads, and the women were deeply moved to see him, but they just crouched beneath their desks amidst the flying vernacular. You see, most artistic firms such as this don't have sturdy furnishings and, oh, several pretty things got broken. Including the contract with the firm. It was time to leave.

What goes up with ease does not always want to come down. The bull saw the stairs and decided to stay. It turned into the proverbial bull-in-a-china-shop waltz. After the pushing and tail twisting and kicking and giging, the bull finally took a step, just one step and slid all the way down the wooden stairs, pealing off the banister, lifting the rungs of several stairs and beating Blue to the door by a frog's hair, sending them both out onto the sidewalk near the Driskill Hotel. And like all things fun, you want to do them again, particularly when there is a bet. Was he really that gentle? Now on level ground, they loaded him up.

Next stop, The Texas Chili Parlour. When the boys led the bull into the restaurant, the manager actually levitated across the counter, spooking the giant black pet. Tables tipped and chairs snapped. No real damage in cowboy terms so they made a hasty exit, along with the manager's orange MGB. You see, it got stuck to the gooseneck trailer and, well it went for a ride, too. In fact, when they were finished it was just about as gentle as that old bull.

Later on all the amends were made, of course, for the harm done and most everybody is still living happily ever after. I know that for a fact and I do know something else about Tom's gregarious love of life: it is an authentic lifestyle. Daily, he commits to the best, to be the best, to do the best and to leave the best behind. Today, like a hundred years ago, I would want him riding with me. Heck, I'd even let him bring that old bull along just for the hell of it. Who in the *world* would stand in our way?

By the code of the west, I remain...

Craig Davis Conlee

Craig Davis Conlee
President & Founder
Fourth Generation Texan

700 S. BRYAN STREET • BRYAN, TEXAS 77803-3928 • 409.775.1611 • FAX: 409.775.1917 • WWW.BRAZOSCF.COM

> " . . . the bull finally took a step, just one step and slid all the way down the wooden stairs . . . "

I asked Craig Conlee to write my "Tall Texas Tale" because: *He's a fourth-generation Texan. His great-grandfather and grandfather were sheriffs of Brazos County and his dad was mayor of Bryan. Craig's a "feller" who can tell an honest Texas tale.*

KRANDEL LEE NEWTON
BUTT SKETCH ARTIST

SKETCHING PEOPLE'S BACKSIDES!

My Texas post is: Butt Sketch Artist to the World, with a special view from Texas.

I came into this world on: August 14, 1958, butt first!

I hang my hat in: Dallas Love Field and DFW Airport.

I'm a real cowboy because: I don't mind putting on my boots and diving into my work.

If you run into my friend Lisa Browing ask her about the time I: Caught on fire while doing a sketch at an engagement party. Apparently the aerosol spray I use to seal my sketches doesn't mix well with burning candles! It was an unforgettable scene. I "stopped, dropped and rolled," somebody sprayed me down with a nearby fire extinguisher, I was yelling, people were staring. When the firemen left and everyone calmed down, there was no question Krandel Lee can really light up a party!

If you walked a mile in my boots: You would see so much tail that you would get worn out!

I love Texas because: Wranglers and Rocky Mountain jeans are in no short supply!

"Knock yourself out!"

—Krandel's Favorite Texas Saying

talk.

Long ago and far away in a distant galaxy far away (Fair Park in Dallas) my bride Murphy and I were seeking shelter from the elements on a day much more typically Irish than Texan at the annual Irish festival.

We ended up huddled in a booth with Tom Stephenson, Janet Mitchell, Sally Francis, Roger Albright, Kyle Weinstein and some of the other usual suspects trying to sell green sunglasses on this very cold and rainy day to help raise money for the lower Greenville avenue St. Patrick's Day Parade. Needless to say our business was more than a little bit slow. Then, after an hour or so of fortifying ourselves with Guinness and watching an Irish wolfhound eat raw potatoes in just two or three bites, our fortunes changed.

A small black man with a grin as large as the blarney stone set up an easel at the booth next door and began hustling the sparse crowd to do their caricature---not from the front, mind you, but from the back.... And that was how we met Krandel Lee Newton, the original butt sketch artist.

He posed his subjects facing away from him and in just a matter of minutes created a professional artwork with just a little extra attention given to the area surrounding the derriere. (Visible panty lines were removed for an extra 2$) The truly amazing thing about his work was that he actually captured the person's personality in his sketches as attested to by friends and family who watched the process with giggles and titters and the obvious jokes about getting a little "behind" in his work.

We swapped cards that day and I convinced the radio station to start including Krandel in our promotional events whenever we did a public broadcast. And then one day he got his big break. Channel 8 did a feature story that CNN picked up and ran every two hours for 24 hours one day about Dallas' "Amazing Butt Sketch" artist. As a result of the publicity, Krandel soon began scheduling appearances near and far as party-planners and then corporations across the country recognized his unique ability to break the ice for their guests.

As it turned out, Krandel is a serious artist and soon galleries were showing his "real" art to the public while one annual "Butt Sketch World Tour" followed another to pay more than just the rent. We all knew he had made the big-time when he had to use some of his money to hire attorneys to quash the inevitable impersonators that tried to take advantage of his fame.

Today, Krandel Lee Newton stands tall as he pursues his talents both in the "serious" art world---and of course----preserving posteriors for posterity. He has his cake and sketches it, too.

Kevin McCarthy
BIG 570 KLIF Radio, Dallas

SUSQUEHANNA
DALLAS/FT. WORTH

3500 Maple Ave | 16th Floor | Dallas, TX 75219
214.526.2400 | fax 214.520.4300 | www.big570.com

"**A small black man with a grin as large as the blarney stone set up an easel ... and began hustling the sparse crowd to do their caricature ...**"

I asked Kevin McCarthy to write my "Tall Texas Tale" because: *Kevin is an extremely talented person who doesn't take himself too seriously, a classic example that's encouraged me to carry out my work tongue-in-cheek!*

CHUCK NORRIS
WALKER, TEXAS RANGER

GEORGE BUSH

May 26, 1999

Dear Martana,

While I have many friends I consider *real* Texas Men, there are few that stand out as well as Chuck Norris. I mean, who else do I know that is a six-time World Karate Champ and World Open Speedboat Champ? Who else could possibly be Walker-Texas Ranger!

From the minute I met Chuck Norris when he so nicely offered to help me in my effort to become President of the United States, I knew I had met a very genuine and caring individual. I enjoyed getting to know him better and was delighted in 1990 when he came to visit me about a life-long dream he had. He wanted to offer needy youngsters in Texas the opportunity to benefit from martial arts training as part of their daily school curriculum. He knew how martial arts could change and re-direct lives, because it had happened to him thirty years earlier.

Chuck credits me for giving him the encouragement he needed, but the truth is his *Kick Drugs Out of America Foundation* has made a huge difference in the lives of Texas kids, and Chuck made it happen.

The program now works with over 3,400 youngsters in 27 schools in Texas, Illinois and Pennsylvania. I am delighted every year when I see many of his "karate kids" show their skills at Chuck's annual fundraising event in Houston.

Chuck is also a very modest guy and six years ago when he invited me to play in his tennis invitational I thought he was being modest when he told me he was a terrible tennis player. Well, I should have realized that real Texas Men don't lie! However, we did play and had a comical time. I hear Chuck tells this story a lot so I am sure he won't mind…a television reporter asked me after our match if I thought Chuck Norris was a good tennis player and my only response since Texas Men don't lie was that Norris is a wonderful guy, totally dedicated to his Foundation. Chuck has never gotten over that gracious response and hasn't played with me since!

Bottom line, Chuck has never let celebrity go to his head. This down to earth modest man is a true "Point of Light" and most definitely a "Real Texas Man". We Texans are lucky that Chuck cares so deeply for our children.

Sincerely,

G. Bush

"**. . . his Kick Drugs Out of America Foundation has made a huge difference in the lives of Texas kids . . .**"

I asked President George Bush to write my "Tall Texas Tale" because: *I consider him a close friend and a man that I look up to.*

Six-Time Karate Champion & World Open Boat Champion

My Texas post is: The set of *Walker, Texas Ranger*.

I came into this world on: My birthday.

I hang my hat in: Dallas, TX.

I'm a real cowboy because: I kiss my horse and pat my woman.

If you run into my friends Bob and Larry ask them about our: Para-sailing business venture in Hawaii! We could not get the para-sail by boat over the water, so we tried it by land with a car. The para-sail went up and Bob got caught in the trees. He crashed to the ground, but fortunately wasn't hurt!

If you walked a mile in my boots: You would have to buy a new pair.

I love Texas because: Texans are real people with a gracious attitude.

"The only time you fail is when you don't learn from the experience."

— Chuck's Favorite Texas Saying

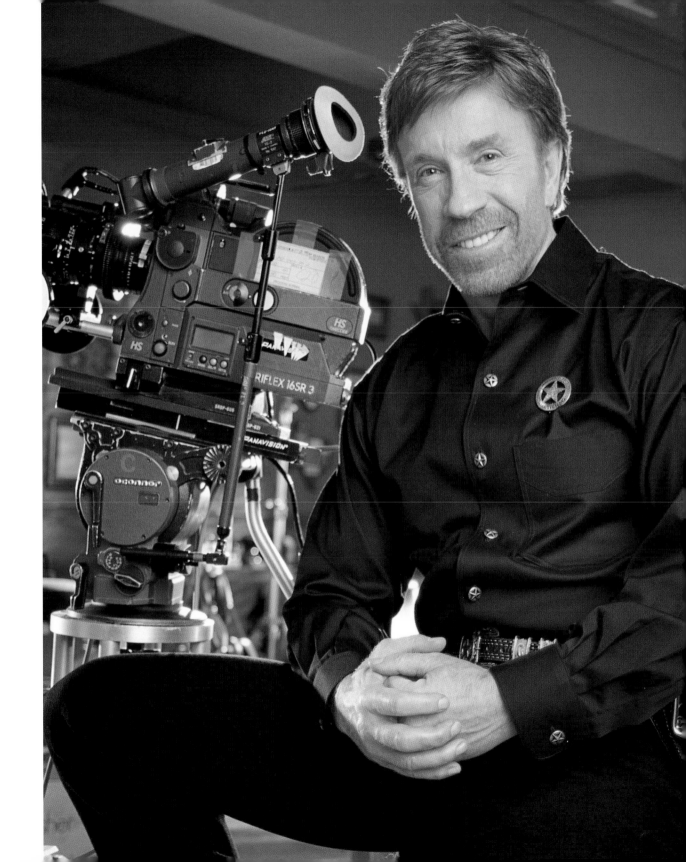

KEVIN PRIGEL
THE ELECTRONIC INVESTOR

STARTED STREETADVISOR.COM WHILE ATTENDING TEXAS CHRISTIAN UNIVERSITY

My Texas post is: StreetAdvisor.com in Fort Worth, TX—a provider of unbiased stock analysis.

I came into this world on: July 14, 1979—in a bull market!

I hang my hat in: Cyberspace.

I'm a real cowboy because: I still prefer getting my hands dirty over a day in the office.

If you run into my friend Matt Kartsonis ask him about the time I: Was just starting my company. I needed some marketing advice. So, while on a long layover in Washington I dropped in unannounced at Amazon.com's Seattle headquarters. I told the secretary I was there to see the Marketing Director, and as luck would have it, I ended up spending half the day with him.

If you walked a mile in my boots: You'd find out why you just want to keep working—you'd never want to quit. I'm just as passionate about the 20th mile as I am about the 1st.

My ultimate Texas date would be: Dinner at the Mansion on Turtle Creek, a plane ride to San Antonio to have a drink on the Riverwalk, then off to South Padre Island to watch the sun rise.

I love Texas because: It's kind of ironic that I spent most of my life in Kansas but had to come to Fort Worth to be in a tornado!

"If the idea is not completely absurd, it is destined for failure."

—Kevin's Favorite Texas Saying

"He was writing software programs at four, selling computer programs by ten, and building Internet portals for companies by fourteen."

I asked Bryan King to write my "Tall Texas Tale" because: *Without him, StreetAdvisor wouldn't have been possible. He taught me a lot about business, but more importantly he taught me what a real ranch looks like.*

LUTHER KING CAPITAL MANAGEMENT
301 COMMERCE STREET, SUITE 1600
FORT WORTH, TEXAS 76102
817/332-3235
METRO 817/429-6256   FAX 817/332-4630

July 25, 2000

Dear Martana,

The Digital Generation, The Internet Generation, The Tech Generation. If these words describe today's college grads, then Kevin Prigel could be the poster boy.

Kevin is simply gifted. He was writing software programs at four, selling computer programs by ten, and building Internet portals for companies by fourteen. He has been called everything from a prodigy to wunderkind.

I first met Kevin when our firm recruited him as an intern from the Texas Christian University finance program. Though only seventeen, Kevin had earned enough college credits in math and science while in his Kansas public high school to start TCU as a junior. While he was already celebrated as a rare intellectual talent what struck me the most was his amazing "dream it-do it" spirit. His creativity and his unrivaled understanding of the technological landscape, provided him with the cornerstones to become a successful entrepreneur.

With a steely work ethic and a super-charged Palm Pilot loaded with business plans, Kevin was clearly a workhorse worth betting on. As he honed his analytical and business skills dissecting our prospective investments, he was constantly tweaking his own start-up ideas. As Kevin neared his twentieth birthday, he had already launched several of his own businesses. We decided that some of his independent projects were right on track and channeled our joint resources behind StreetAdvisor.com.

But don't think for a minute that Kevin's 24/7 work life doesn't make room for a "Tall Texas Tale" or two. You see, a few years ago I took Kevin along for a bird hunt with a few of my buddies. We all knew that it was his first hunt. We gave him plenty of space away from the group so he wouldn't accidentally shoot one of us. At first he shot a couple of rounds-but missed bird after bird. At the end of the hunt we left Kevin out in the field to keep shooting while we went to clean our guns. Just as Kevin approached us, a dove flew by and Kevin pulled up his gun and shot it down from a pretty good distance. We were all amazed and asked, "How did you do that? You are supposed to be a beginner!" Kevin replied, "Well, I have had some time to figure out the trajectory and did a vector analysis on the angle vs. the..." Needless to say, he continues to impress us both off and on the professional field.

Perhaps the most remarkable thing about Texas Man Kevin Prigel is his ability to take his indepth knowledge of technology and finance and explain it in a way even your grandmother could understand. In these dynamic times when new businesses are started daily, Kevin is able to recognize new technology businesses that will flourish into the future, even if they are brushed off as too uncertain today.

Sincerely,

J. Bryan King

J. Bryan King

STYLLE READ

WESTERN MURALIST

PAINTING BIG WESTERN MURALS & ARTWORK IN FAMOUS TEXAS JOINTS & ACROSS THE BORDER!

My Texas post is: Painting in museums, restaurants and home murals all over the state, plus ranches from Fort Worth to Marfa.

I came into this world on: March 17, 1953, with a palette and brush in my hand.

I was born & raised in: Born in Lufkin, TX and raised in Lufkin, Tyler and pretty much around Fort Worth.

I hang my hat in: Johnson County on the edge of Cleburne.

I'm a real cowboy because: I don't make a living as a cowboy but I've experienced the work and "paint the romance."

If you run into my friend Alpine Business Man Bill Ivey ask him about the time: I opened "Chili with Stylle." He provided the ground and I created a colorful and spicy experience for the town folk. During my formative years in Terlingua, I also floated the Rio Grande regularly and was a desert rat. I still have my foot in Terlingua too, where I am restoring a rock house for the next 99 years with the good graces of Bill and his wife Lisa.

If you walked a mile in my boots: Your boot prints would be in color.

My ultimate Texas date would be: With my favorite Texas gal cutting a rug on the riverwalk in San Antonio.

I love Texas because: Of the different cultures from music, art, architecture and folklore around the state.

"Careful as a naked man climbing a barbed-wire fence."

—Stylle's Favorite Texas Saying

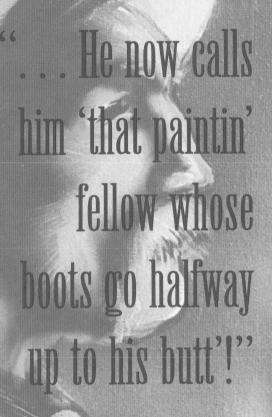

" . . . He now calls him 'that paintin' fellow whose boots go halfway up to his butt'!"

I asked David Tinsley to write my "Tall Texas Tale" because: David is a true Texan and the only man I know who documented traveling around the border of the state of Texas on the ground—he hiked, floated the river, canoed, biked, walked . . .

COYOTE-CROW PRODUCTIONS

Star Route 70, Box 504
Terlinqua. Tx. 79852

MARTANA,

BACK ABOUT A DECADE AGO, I CHANGED AND REMODELED A RESTAURANT I OWNED IN TYLER, TEXAS. WE WANTED TO GIVE DEEP EAST TEXAS A LOOK AT DEEPEST WEST TEXAS, THEIR TRANS PECOS COUNTERPARTS. WE NAMED THE RESTAURANT "CHISOS". I CALLED MY OLE FRIEND STYLLE READ TO GIVE ME SOME IDEAS AND TO PUT HIS TALENT TO USE ON AN EIGHT FOOT HIGH SOLID BOARD FENCE. WE HAD THE BAR LOOKING LIKE A MEXICAN CANTINA AND WE NEEDED THE SAME LOOK ON THE FENCE AND BUILDING OUTSIDE THAT WAS FACING THE LOOP. STYLLE, AS USUAL, DID A REAL NUMBER ON EVERYTHING HE PAINTED-- MOUNTAINS, CACTI, DONKEYS, AND LOTS OF REAL DETAILED STUFF. THIS CREATED LOTS OF INTEREST AND CONVERSATION IN TYLER. ABOUT TWO WEEKS AFTER STYLLE FINISHED THE JOB, A MAN CAME IN CHISOS AND IDENTIFIED HIMSELF AS THE ANIMAL CONTROL OFFICER AND ASKED IF WE HAD SEEN ANY DONKEYS RUNNING AROUND THE LOOP. HE SAID A LADY FROM BULLARD HAD CALLED AND REPORTED BURROS RUNNING LOOSE ON THE LOOP AT OLD BULLARD ROAD. HE CAUGHT ME OFF GUARD, AND THEN I LAUGHED AND PROUDLY SHOWED HIM STYLLE'S ART. I KNEW AT THAT MOMENT STYLLE HAD DONE HIS JOB. HE CREATED A WEST TEXAS "FREE RANGE".

THERE'S AN "OLE RATTLESNAKE" (AND I SAY THAT AFFECTIONATELY) OUT IN SOUTH BREWSTER COUNTY WHOSE REAL NAME IS REX IVEY. REX WAS, IN HIS OWN WORDS, IN THE "COMMISSIONER BUSINESS"-- IN OTHER WORDS, HE WAS A COUNTY COMMISSIONER. I HAVE NEVER HEARD REX CALL ANYONE BY THEIR GIVEN NAME. HE HAD A PENCHANT FOR GIVING PEOPLE NICKNAMES-- "COYOTE", "FANCY PANTS", "DOUBLE NAUGHT", "BANDIT", AND "WOMAN WHO TALKS". BECAUSE I USED TO FLY TO LAJITAS IN A DC-3, HE CALLED ME "AIRPLANE MAN", BUT HIS FAVORITE NAME FOR FOLKS WHO WERE ARTISTS, CREATIVE, OR HAD NO STEADY JOB WAS "BIRDBRAIN". BEFORE HE EVEN KNEW WHAT STYLLE DID FOR A LIVING, HE CALLED HIM "BIRDBRAIN FELLOW WHO WEARS HIS BOOTS HALFWAY UP TO HIS BUTT". REX HAD NOT EVER SEEN ANY OF STYLLE'S WORK. HOWEVER, LATER ON, STYLLE HAD THE OPPORTUNITY TO CAPTURE REX IN STYLE. REX AND HIS SON BILL IVEY BOUGHT AND RESTORED THE "GHOST TOWN" IN TERLINGUA. ANGIE "RICA" DEAN HAS A GREAT NIGHTSPOT IN THE OLD MOVIE THEATRE CALLED "STARLIGHT DINNER THEATER". THE STARLIGHT NAME WAS FITTING BECAUSE FOR YEARS THE OLD ADOBE THEATRE HAD NO ROOF! AFTER THE ROOF WAS PUT BACK ON, ANGIE COMMISSIONED STYLLE TO PUT SOME LIFE BACK INTO THE OLD MOVIE SCREEN. HE MADE THE CAMPFIRE SCENE UNDER THE STARS, WHICH IS NOW FAMOUS. WHEN YOU WALK IN THE DOOR, YOUR EYES ARE DRAWN TO THIS SCENE. AFTER A FEW DRINKS AT THE BAR, YOU LOOK AT THE CAMPFIRE, THE STARS AND THE FOLKS AROUND THE FIRE AND YOU CAN SEE THE "OLE RATTLESNAKE" HIMSELF BY THE CAMPFIRE WITH A "EVERYTHING IS RIGHT WITH THE WORLD" LOOK. AFTER REX SAW STYLLE'S WORK, HE NOW CALLS HIM "THAT PAINTIN' FELLOW WHOSE BOOTS GO HALFWAY UP TO HIS BUTT"!

DAVID TINSLEY

PHIL ROMANO
CONCEPTOR & RESTAURATEUR

DOING THINGS DIFFERENTLY!

My Texas post is: Dallas, TX as Founder & CEO of Eatzi's, Nick & Sam's, Fuddruckers, Cozymel's, Macaroni Grill, Rudy's, NachoMama's, Rosalie's Cocina, etc.

I came into this world on: October 12, 1939—ten minutes before lunch.

I hang my hat in: Dallas, TX.

I'm a real cowboy because: I got married in Texas and had my only child in Texas—and also I have sand in my boots.

If you run into my friend Mo ask him about the time I: Punched and knocked out a horse!

If you walked a mile in my boots: You'd be tired.

I love Texas because: Texas embraces all that I do!

"I might as well do it. I can't when I'm dead."

— Phil's Favorite Texas Saying

Norman E. Brinker
Chairman of the Board

BRINKER
INTERNATIONAL.

Dear Martana:

Few men I have met in my business career exemplify the Texas entrepreneurial spirit like Philip Romano. He is a pioneer of ideas and one of the great innovators in restaurant history. Phil has been wise enough to pick the Lone Star State as a launch point for all of his national successes, which include Fuddrucker's, Romano's Macaroni Grill, Eatzi's and other great chains.

A first generation Italian from New York, Phil has found his niche in Texas, where he has spent his last 23 years whipping up some of the best grub this side of the Red River. As founder of Steak & Ale and Chairman of Brinker International, the parent company of Chili's Grill & Bar, Romano's Macaroni Grill, On The Border, Cozymel's, Eatzi's, Maggiano's Little Italy, and Corner Bakery, I've had the privilege of working with some talented people over the years, but Phil always seems to be ahead of the curve. I believe he thinks "outside the box" better than just about anybody in the industry.

I can safely say from experience that Phil is his own man. Not long after he launched Fuddrucker's in San Antonio in the early 1980's, I stopped by to see him and was fascinated by his upscale hamburger concept. I was told that he was out of the country and rarely returned calls. And he didn't...until nearly a decade later! Fuddrucker's had been a huge sensation and now Phil was starting to realize a similar potential for Macaroni Grill. But he didn't want to expand it himself this time, so he phoned me and said in a calm voice, "Norman, this is Phil Romano returning your call." I said, "Doggone it Phil, that was ten years ago!"

In less than three weeks after speaking to him, the Brinker team visited Phil at Macaroni Grill and soon afterwards, we negotiated a lasting arrangement with him. Phil has truly been an independent idea man for Brinker ever since. He went on to launch Cozymel's, Spageddies, and Eatzi's, which are all in Texas, plus a half dozen or so other restaurants in the state.

Is Phil irreverent? Obviously. Is he politically correct? No way! But Phil operates with a fearlessness and confidence that makes him the envy of his contemporaries. He's always quick with a joke, which he delivers in his typical wry tone. Phil has also quietly given money to support fledgling artists and has assisted family and friends with various ventures. He firmly believes in the philosophy of giving back.

Phil remains a living Texas legend with a zest for life, a passion for his business, and a sense of dignity, ethics and honor that are reflected in his restaurants and in his life. Now that he and his lovely wife, Lillie, have a young son, Phil has decided to forgo early retirement and remain in Texas to ply his trade and launch his concepts as young Sam attends school.

Texas will certainly benefit from his decision to continue developing exciting concepts.

Sincerely,

Norman

Norman Brinker

6820 LBJ Freeway   Dallas, Texas 75240-6515   972 980-9917
www.brinker.com

" ... 'Norman, this is Phil Romano returning your call.' I said, 'Doggone it Phil, that was ten years ago!' "

I asked Norman Brinker to write my "Tall Texas Tale" because: *He's a respected colleague and friend.*

DARRELL ROYAL
LEGENDARY UT COACH

COACHED THREE NATIONAL UNIVERSITY OF TEXAS CHAMPIONSHIPS

(I CAN'T TAKE CREDIT FOR IT ALL. IT WAS A COMBINATION OF THE PLAYERS AND THE OTHER COACHES THAT MADE IT HAPPEN. IT WAS ALWAYS A TEAM EFFORT. ALWAYS.)

My Texas post is: Assistant to the President, University of Texas Athletic Affairs.

I came into this world on: July 6, 1924—yellin', "How do I get out of here?"

I hang my hat in: Austin, TX—where I can turn 360 degrees and see new wood. There are new houses going up everywhere! When I first came to Austin, there was just the University and the state capitol. Now the place is full of "Dellionaires!"

I'm a real cowboy because: There's nothin' cowboy about me. I don't ride horses or wear boots or drink Lone Star beer. The thing that qualifies me is that I love Bob Wills country music.

If you run into my friends: You will find they are not all rich and not all poor. I had a friend that wrote "I dwelled with Kings, I dwelled with bums, I am in your church and I am in your slums. I am music. I am everywhere." This expresses how I feel about my friends. I have friends from 7-11 employees to President Johnson. I don't pick my friends for their position in life.

If you walked a mile in my boots: It would probably be boring, but it was a hell of a ride getting here—you should have caught me earlier!

I love Texas because: Texas has accepted me. I was embraced by many kind people, and my life in Texas has been a pleasure.

"When you pass three things can happen to ya, and two of them are bad!"

—Darrell's Favorite Texas Saying

"—Coach Royal just watched."
"Then, all at once it happened . . ."

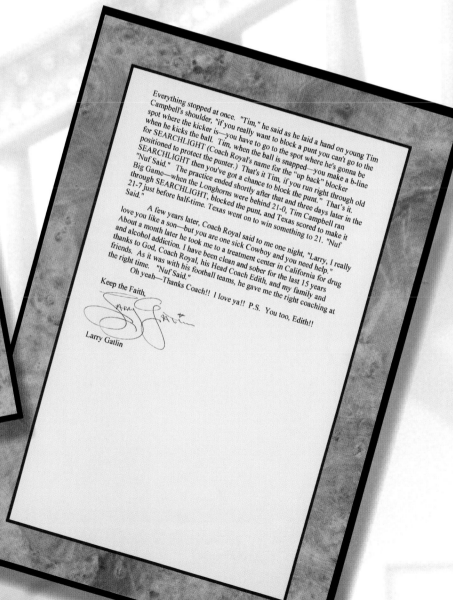

LARRY GATLIN

"Nuf Said"

A few years ago a cute-as-a-bug, but slightly confused, 8-year-old boy placed his sawed-off 9-iron into his golf bag, unstrapped it and took it off the golf cart. "Dad" he said, "I really love you, but I can't do this anymore—you've told me to swing slow, swing hard, turn my hand over, keep my arm straight. Dad I just can't remember all that stuff." There was a pregnant pause and then he continued, "Besides, I don't want to do anything in my life that makes me as mad as golf makes you." He then shouldered the bag, walked to the Pro-Shop and called his mom to come and get him. Another Product of Too Much Coaching and Not Enough Cheerleading!!! (By the way—the kid took up the game 11 years later on his own and is 2 handicap at Barton Creek Golf Club in Austin).

You probably guessed it—I, Larry Gatlin, was the Too Much Coaching, Not Enough Cheerleading, Overbearing Dad-Golf Coach. "Nuf Said." And the cute-as-a-bug 8-year-old is my son Josh. But enough about the Gatlin Boys, let's get to the hero of the story.

Along about the same time as the Too Much Coaching incident, I had another "Nuf Said" experience—I was invited by then new friend Coach Darrell Royal to attend a Longhorn Football practice 3 days before the Bluebonnet Bowl Game in Houston against the Colorado Buffaloes, coached by another good friend, Coach Eddie Crowder.

Anyway, I was really excited. I was ready to see the legendary Coach, up close and personal. We stood on the field together and watched the young men jogging and stretching and passing and warming up. The team then divided into offense and defense and the assistant coaches began doing their deal—Coach Royal just watched. The players continued their drills and the assistants did more of their deal—Coach Royal just watched. I was, needless to say, more than slightly disappointed. I wanted to see some of Darrel Royal's legendary coaching skills!! I wanted to see some strategy and some "do this and do that" and "throw it like this and tackle like that" stuff. But no—Coach Royal just watched. Bummer. (He didn't even have a whistle.) There was no fist pounding—his arms remained crossed most of the time. There were no shouts of anger. No (expletive deleted) curse words, and there was (expletive deleted) sure no player choking, Bobby Knight!! Coach Royal just watched. Double Bummer. How did this guy get into the Hall of Fame? Then, all at once it happened—Coach Royal quietly with no fanfare or whistle blowing walked over to where his life-long friend Coach Mike Campbell was working with the Punt Block Team—hold on just a minute fellas—God had finally spoken.

Everything stopped at once. "Tim," he said as he laid a hand on young Tim Campbell's shoulder, "if you really want to block a punt you can't go to the spot where the kicker is—you have to go to the spot where he's gonna be when he kicks the ball. Tim, when the ball is snapped—you make a b-line for SEARCHLIGHT (Coach Royal's name for the "up back" blocker positioned to protect the punter.) That's it Tim, if you run right through old SEARCHLIGHT then you've got a chance to block the punt." That's it. "Nuf Said." The practice ended shortly after that and three days later in the Big Game—when the Longhorns were behind 21-0, Tim Campbell ran through SEARCHLIGHT, blocked the punt, and Texas scored to make it 21-7 just before half-time. Texas went on to win something to 21. "Nuf Said."

A few years later, Coach Royal said to me one night, "Larry, I really love you like a son—but you are one sick Cowboy and you need help." About a month later he took me to a treatment center in California for drug and alcohol addiction. I have been clean and sober for the last 15 years thanks to God, Coach Royal, his Head Coach Edith, and my family and friends. As it was with his football teams, he gave me the right coaching at the right time. "Nuf Said."

Oh yeah—Thanks Coach!! I love ya!! P.S. You too, Edith!!

Keep the Faith,

Larry Gatlin

Larry Gatlin

I asked Larry Gatlin to write my "Tall Texas Tale" because: *I just played golf with him. He's a good friend and I knew he'd lie for me. And he's a big football fan.*

JOHNNY RUTHERFORD
"LONE STAR J.R.", OPEN WHEEL LEGEND

THREE-TIME "INDY 500" WINNER '74, '76 & '80

My Texas post is: Johnny Rutherford Inc., Director of Special Events for Indy Racing League.

I came into this world on: December 3, 1938. FAST.

I hang my hat in: Fort Worth, TX—next to my helmet.

I'm a real cowboy because: I love to live in Texas!

If you run into my friend A.J. Foyt ask him about the time I: Spun a 360 in front of him on the track—five times in one season! I never did wreck and A.J. would always say, "How'd you do that?"

If you walked a mile in my boots: You would "Go Fast & Turn Left" and you would need a seat belt!

I love Texas because: It's the last frontier, and where the "West Begins."

"Nobody ever remembers who finished second."

—Johnny's Favorite Texas Saying

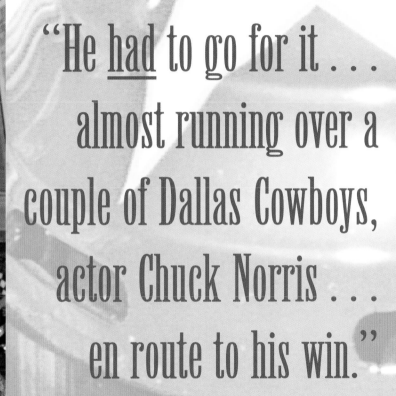

"He <u>had</u> to go for it . . . almost running over a couple of Dallas Cowboys, actor Chuck Norris . . . en route to his win."

I asked Eddie Gossage to write my "Tall Texas Tale" because: *He is a very astute individual, the general manager of Texas Motor Speedway and is very knowledgeable about racing.*

OFFICE OF THE GENERAL MANAGER

January 20, 1998

Dear Martana:

Texas men are *real* men. In certain sports, only *real* men can be successful. When you combine a Texas man with a sport for real men, well you inevitably come up with a guy like "Lone Star JR" -- Johnny Rutherford. He's a Texas man in a real man's sport and he's been on top of the motorsports world by winning three Indy 500s.

Unlike another real man from Texas -- a Houston rattlesnake named A.J. Foyt -- Rutherford's looks and style somehow contradicted his success in this life-and-death battle to be master of steel-and-chrome on asphalt. Sure he was as tough, mean and competitive as Foyt. But there he stood in Victory Lane at Indy after racing 500 miles and his uniform had *perfect* creases, his hair was *perfectly* coifed and his teeth *perfectly* white. You would swear that he could have just as easily stepped from the pulpit as he did from the cockpit of a fire-breathing, methanol burning 600-horsepower needle-nosed rocket he called a race car. And the world loved him!

From the time he climbed into a race car on the dirt oval at Devil's Bowl Speedway just outside of Dallas all the way to the top of the racing world, Fort Worth's Johnny Rutherford just didn't look the part. But don't believe it -- he is the real thing. The competitive fire still burns. Last April, during the opening weekend of our inaugural season, the first race we held was the Troy Aikman Stars & Celebrities charity race. Unlike the big NASCAR stock cars that ran later in the weekend, an assortment of sports, entertainment, media and political personalities staged a race in Legends Cars. These half-scale replicas of 1940 modified sedans and coupes are a hand-full but not as serious as the real thing. Rutherford was running third with a couple of laps to go when it dawned on him that the winner of Aikman's celebrity race would go into the record books as the winner of the first event ever at America's second-largest sports facility. He *had* to go for it and he did, almost running over a couple of Dallas Cowboys, actor Chuck Norris and gymnast Bart Conner en route to his win. The race paid $1 million or so less than Indy (actually, the winner received only a trophy), but ol' J.R. ran as hard as he ever did at the Brickyard. The fire still burns!

I can think of my own list of real Texas men, and when I do my list has to include three-time Indy 500 winner -- and the winner of the first race ever at Texas Motor Speedway -- Fort Worth's own Johnny Rutherford!

Best Regards,

Eddie Gossage

Eddie Gossage
Executive Vice President
and General Manager

Texas Motor Speedway • P.O. Box 500 • Fort Worth, Texas 76101-2500
Administration (817) 215-8580 • Fax (817) 215-8525
A DIVISION OF SPEEDWAY MOTORSPORTS, INC. A NYSE COMPANY.

KENNETH E. SALYER, M.D.
INTERNATIONAL CRANIOFACIAL PLASTIC SURGEON

TREATED CHILDREN FROM OVER 60 COUNTRIES REGARDLESS OF THEIR ABILITY TO PAY

My Texas post is: International Craniofacial Plastic & Reconstructive Surgery in Dallas, TX.

I came into this world on: A "wing and a prayer" on a hot day in August 1936 when there was no managed care and the hospital stay was ten days at a cost of two dollars a day!

I hang my hat in: Dallas & Telluride, Colorado.

I'm a real cowboy because: I am in the saddle everyday, dealing "head-on" with the challenges of creating new faces for children and influencing their lives.

If you run into my friend Herman Cestero in Puerto Rico ask him about the time we: Were in his runaway boat going at top speed, and the engine wouldn't slow down or turn off. He finally ran into (and over) the dock to make it stop. You should have seen the people running in all directions when they saw us coming!

If you walked a mile in my boots: You would feel the joy of caring for those with facial deformity and creating new faces and opportunities for their lives.

I love Texas because: It's a special wide-open place, where development of the International Craniofacial Institute was made possible by the friendliness, caring, support and environment of the "can-do-anything attitude"—that's Texas.

"You won't know until you try!"

— Kenneth's Favorite Texas Saying

SERVICIO DE CIRUGIA PLASTICA Y RECONSTRUCTIVA

Hospital "Manuel Gea González"

Calzada de Tlalpan 4800, México, D. F. 14000 Tel. 525/ 665 5440

Fax 525/ 652 0807 E-mail fortizm@dfi.telmex.net.mx

November, 1999

Martana
Texas Men

Dear Martana:

I met Ken Salyer many years ago in Paris. He was then a young Plastic Surgeon interested in learning the new techniques on Craniofacial Surgery developed by Paul Tessier.

Since that time he has become one of the world's experts in that field. His numerous scientific publications have contributed to a better understanding and improved treatment of congenital craniofacial malformations.

Because of our common professional interest, I have developed a close friendship with Ken over the years. I have had the opportunity to follow his career, to appreciate his generous dedication to his patients and his family as well as his permanent interest in research and teaching. As a result of his endeavours Ken is now an international authority in his field.

He is also a gifted amateur photographer and a good sport. When he was my guest in our country home by the lake in Valle de Bravo, I took him in my small sail boat to photo-graph the start of a sailing race. Once at the starting line we decided to take part in the race. We did well on the windward leg in spite of the fact that Ken had no experience in sailing. Rounding the mark in a difficult manoeuvre, we capsized the boat without any personal injuries but with irreparable damage to Ken's fancy photo equipment. As expected, with his bonhomie and a sense of humor, Ken accepted the event as an enjoyable learning experience.

It has been a privilege to know Ken Salyer, to work with him in scientific and teaching projects and to enjoy his gener-ous friendship. He is certainly a very tall Texan.

Cordially yours,

FERNANDO ORTIZ MONASTERIO, M.D.
PROFESSOR EMERITUS

I asked Fernando Ortiz Monasterio, M.D. to write my "Tall Texas Tale" because: *He is my compadre, whom I shared many professional and personal experiences with around the world.*

" . . . we capsized the boat without any personal injuries but with irreparable damage to Ken's fancy photo equipment."

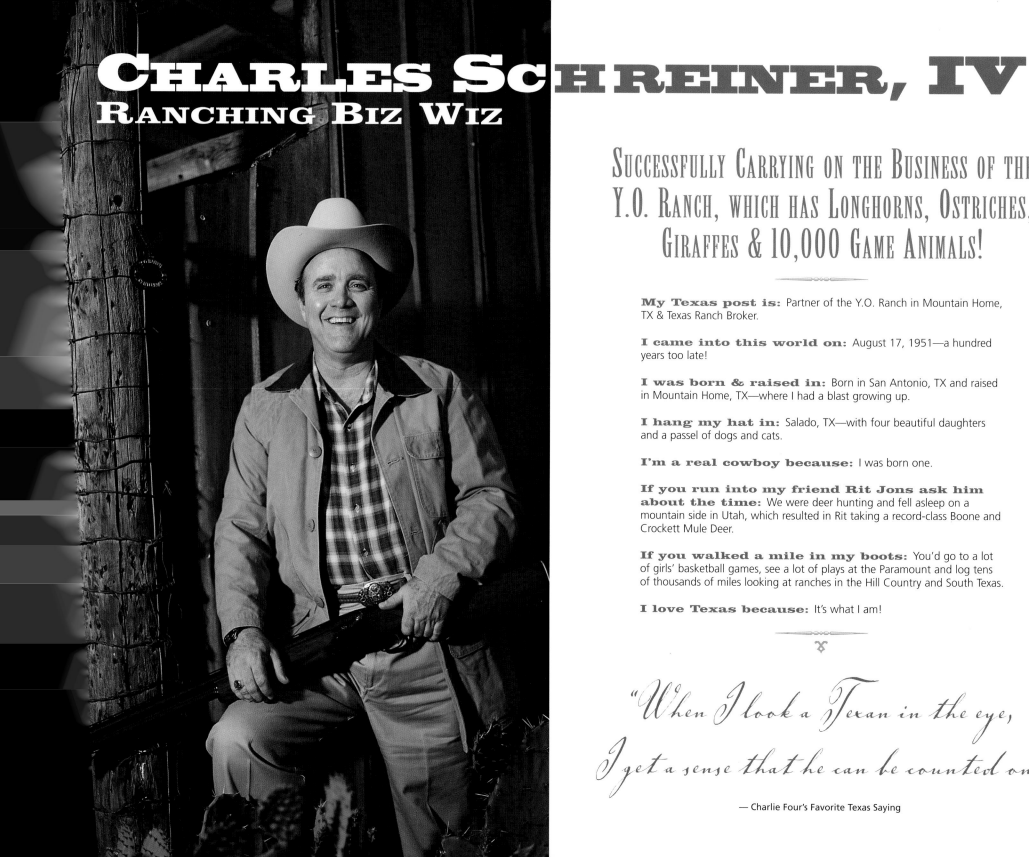

CHARLES SCHREINER, IV
RANCHING BIZ WIZ

SUCCESSFULLY CARRYING ON THE BUSINESS OF THE Y.O. RANCH, WHICH HAS LONGHORNS, OSTRICHES, GIRAFFES & 10,000 GAME ANIMALS!

My Texas post is: Partner of the Y.O. Ranch in Mountain Home, TX & Texas Ranch Broker.

I came into this world on: August 17, 1951—a hundred years too late!

I was born & raised in: Born in San Antonio, TX and raised in Mountain Home, TX—where I had a blast growing up.

I hang my hat in: Salado, TX—with four beautiful daughters and a passel of dogs and cats.

I'm a real cowboy because: I was born one.

If you run into my friend Rit Jons ask him about the time: We were deer hunting and fell asleep on a mountain side in Utah, which resulted in Rit taking a record-class Boone and Crockett Mule Deer.

If you walked a mile in my boots: You'd go to a lot of girls' basketball games, see a lot of plays at the Paramount and log tens of thousands of miles looking at ranches in the Hill Country and South Texas.

I love Texas because: It's what I am!

"When I look a Texan in the eye, I get a sense that he can be counted on."

— Charlie Four's Favorite Texas Saying

BRENHAM NATIONAL BANK
MEMBER BRENHAM BANCSHARES, INC.
2211 SOUTH DAY STREET
P.O. BOX 2568
BRENHAM, TEXAS 77834-2568
409-836-4571, 1-888-292-4571
FAX # 409-836-1408, 409-836-4398
www.bnbank.com

May 26, 1999

Dear Martana,

If there is a characteristic that makes Texas Men unique, it is a combination of toughness embodying self-reliance, blended with a compassionate sense of honor to do the right thing.

I don't think a better example can be found than the fourth generation scion of one of Texas oldest and best known families - Charles Schreiner, IV. He symbolizes a family that civilized and made productive a large part of the Texas hill country. His namesake, Captain Charles Schreiner, left Alsace-Lorraine and assembled a ranch of 550,000 acres in the 1880's calling it the YO. "Four" as he is called by his friends, not only carried on the ranching tradition, but helped expand the image and involvements of the ranch including its preeminence as a world renown exotic hunting facility, a state of the art taxidermy operation, a children's camp, and a cherished logo that even adorns a Dallas west end restaurant. Dewar's Scotch was so impressed with "Four" that they put his face, name, and accomplishments in magazine advertisements and on billboards. However, while the billboard image conveyed the handshake and smile, it could not capture the heart and mind that are what makes Charlie IV a true Texas man.

In the years I have been privileged to know him we have annually co-sponsored two events. One, an annual gathering of worldwide friends at the ranch, known as the "YO Gathering" that is often best remembered by Charlie IV's special bus tours that led a former insurance commissioner to note, "And they wonder why insurance goes up." While another noted, "I see why people feel close to God out here." His tradition of leaving people at the gate running after the bus ended when Mike Hopkins said nothing, but stuck him with a $600 restaurant bill six months later with a "gotcha."

The other event is a father-son hunt each December at the YO. It started with Charlie taking his daughters and with me taking my son Tee. His interest in children is renown and he and his wife, Mary Helen, are devoted to the Peaceable Kingdom Retreat for children; so it wasn't unusual for him to "adopt" Tee to teach him to shoot and hunt. It was a blessing for me since both Tee and Charlie were left-handed. The problem started when he began teaching Tee to drive his "tank-like" Suburban safari hunting style through the brush, always encouraging him to be more bold and take on bigger brush since Tee was young and hesitant. Wanting to please, Tee bent his head, pushed on the gas, and headed for a sizable post oak tree since Charlie had made no distinction. By the time Charlie pushed the wheel and brake, I was on the floor of the back seat and we were in a ravine well on our way to two flat tires. Charlie noted, "Well, I think we have taught Tee a valuable lesson today." Tee has never forgotten it, nor have I, but it serves as a testament to Charlie's drive to help others, live life to the fullest, and to keep the "wild west" tradition alive.

Best regards,

Skipper

Tieman H. Dippel, Jr.
Chairman

"The problem started when he began teaching Tee to drive his 'tank-like' Suburban safari hunting style through the brush . . ."

I asked Skipper Dippel to write my "Tall Texas Tale" because: *I had a pretty good idea that he'd do a bang up job . . . what with his stellar reputation for spinning some of the most outrageous Texas yarns!*

JAKE SHULMAN
E-COMMERCE ARCHITECT

FINANCIAL OPERATIONS "WIZARD"!

My Texas post is: E-commerce central—my office in Houston, TX.

I came into this world on: January 9, 1970, with hope and a dream.

I was born & raised in: Houston, TX, the "former" home of the Oilers.

I hang my hat in: Downtown Houston, TX for the night life.

I'm a cowboy at heart because: I have down-to-earth Texas values.

If you run into my friend Will Ulbricht ask him about the time I: Helped him clean out his barn. We were going out of town for a supposed hunting trip, but after we got out to the country I found out our "hunting trip" was a ruse. Bill actually just needed some help cleaning out an old barn!

If you walked a mile in my boots: You would have traveled the world many times over.

My ultimate Texas date would be: Cocktails to get the conversation flowing, and then a romantic candlelight dinner at Tony's.

I love Texas because: People from Texas are down-to-earth and real—not plastic and fake.

"Give me a place to stand and I will move the world."

— Jake's Favorite Texas Saying

VAN McFARLAND & ASSOCIATES
ATTORNEYS AT LAW
SUITE 4600
1100 LOUISIANA STREET
HOUSTON, TEXAS 77002-5281

TELEPHONE (713) 650-0150
TELECOPIER (713) 650-0146

December 3, 1999

Dear Ms. Martana,

I have known Jake Shulman and his mother Carolyn Farb for many years. Jake was born in Houston in 1970. He is named after his great-grandfather, "Jake" Freedman, one of the pioneers of Las Vegas and founder of the Sands Hotel and Casino.

Jake is the founder and CEO of E-Commerce Edge, Inc. based in Houston, Texas. He seems to have business acumen rare for his age. Jake works long hours and reads over a thousand pages a week to keep abreast of emerging trends and technologies.

Jake is an outdoorsman and an athlete. He loves the challenge of the black diamond ski trails in Colorado and he scuba dives all over the world. He enjoys entertaining and likes to barbecue for his friends. Jake keeps fit daily at the University Club in Houston.

Jake's mother, Carolyn, the Texas philanthropist, has supported innumerable worthwhile causes, and Jake has inherited this admirable trait.

Last year Jake got a Black Lab puppy he named Prince. Prince used to think Jake could sing. Now they sing together.

Sincerely,

Van McFarland

Van McFarland

"Jake . . . reads over a thousand pages a week . . ."

I asked Van McFarland to write my "Tall Texas Tale" because: *It was the only time I could get an attorney to do something for free!*

JOE SIERRA
TIGUA "INDIAN JOE"

HELPING MY TRIBE PRESERVE OUR MOST IMPORTANT ASSETS—OUR TRADITIONS, OUR FUTURE GENERATIONS & BECOMING SELF-SUFFICIENT IN THE MODERN WORLD

My Texas post is: El Paso, TX, El Paso Film Commission, where I assist in finding great locations for movies such as *Lone Wolf McQuade*, *Courage Under Fire* and *Last Man Standing*, to name a few.

I came into this world on: October 29, 1943, looking at a beautiful blue sky.

I was born & raised in: Ysleta, TX, El Paso County on the Tigua Indian Reservation.

I hang my hat "bandana" in: El Paso, TX, Ysleta del Sur Pueblo, where I enjoy cooking meals like my famous red chili with fresh Indian bread and sharing it with my friends and grandkids.

I'm a real Indian because: Now I am teaching our children the way our grandfathers taught, with dignity and respect for our elders. I am proud of where I came from.

If you run into my friend Chuck Norris ask him about the time: He had a simple but great meal on the reservation at my home!

If you walked a mile in my boots: You would see two countries, three states and go to places where you can have peace of mind and enjoy Mother Earth.

I love Texas because: It is true what they say: "Everything is big in Texas"—such as the great big hearts of the many Texans who come from all different ethnic backgrounds. Texas is a country within itself!

As my grandmother always told me,

"Never forget where you came from."

—Joe's Favorite Texas Saying

"... tribal tradition ranks high in Sierra's heart, thus making his decisions stern in the ways of the grandfathers."

I asked Tribal Governor Albert Alvidrez to write my "Tall Texas Tale" because:

He is such a great leader for our modern world and has improved the quality of living for our people.

Ysleta Del Sur Pueblo
Tribal Council
119 S. Old Pueblo Rd. • (915) 859-7913 • El Paso, Texas 79907

Joe Sierra
Ysleta del Sur Pueblo Tribal Judge

"Injun Joe" a.k.a Joe Sierra is one of Texas' best-kept secrets and Ysleta del Sur Pueblo's heart and soul. Judge Sierra, as he is known these days on the reservation, has been extremely instrumental in bringing a flurry of positive attention to our small pueblo in El Paso, Texas. Former tribal governor and now a long time location scout for the El Paso Film Commission, Judge Sierra guides visitors through El Paso's historic sites and gives a taste of tribal tradition, culture and lore. If you're lucky enough, you might even experience a history lesson on the art of bread baking and sample some of his infamous piping red hot chili stew, which is world renowned for its savoring taste.

Another feather in Joe's entourage of talents is his unique connection to the tribal population. As traditional judge, Sierra hears all traditional cases ranging from thefts of venerated objects to sacrilege. With over 360 years of historical perspective on the El Paso valley, tribal tradition ranks high in Sierra's heart, thus making his decisions stern in the ways of the grandfathers.

While there are no formal hotels on the reservation, consider Judge Sierra's hospitality second to none. It is not uncommon upon first introduction to be invited as an overnight guest to the Sierra's home and enjoy a traditional family experience. Home cooking is definitely a treat at this house. Traditional meals such as chile colorado, sopa de pan, and oven-baked biscochos are among some of the Judge's specialties.

After a Tigua welcome and a plentiful traditional meal, you might get lucky and enjoy a story or two about life as a pueblo Indian before federal recognition. Judge Sierra counts endless tales of the hunting and fishing days for the pueblo Indians when life was much slower and peaceful.

So when visiting the westernmost edge of Texas, forget not to visit the Ysleta del Sur Pueblo and sample this rare, authentic way of life. Judge Sierra is sure to give you a hospitable welcome.

Albert Alvidrez, Tribal Governor
Ysleta del Sur Pueblo

STRAN T SMITH
MR. 20X WRANGLER

RODEO'S POSTER BOY

My Texas post is: My country castle on wheels—a horse trailer.

I came into this world on: July 14, 1970—my mom was just about due with me and she was at home alone. She heard someone breaking into the house, so she ran to the barn to hide, but the robbers chased her to the barn! So she jumped on her horse to escape, but as she was riding, she had a pain, and as she jumped off the horse, she went into labor—the horse then went into labor too and had a colt. She had me, got back on the horse and I got on the colt—I have been riding ever since!

I was born & raised in: Tell, TX—we have a baptist church, a post office, and a cotton gin!

I hang my hat in: Tell, TX, and in my trailer the other 300 days of the year when I am on the road.

I'm a real cowboy because: I am a cowboy and Texan because it's in my blood. My Grandad, Dad and brother taught me what being a real cowboy is. I am a cowboy just because I am.

If you run into my brother Smitty ask him about the time I: Drove through Denver during 5:00 o'clock rush hour with a five-horse trailer when I was only twelve years old.

If you walked a mile in my boots: You'd see how blessed I've been. I feel like God has smiled on me all around. Everyday is a new opportunity and I am very thankful I have a chance to get my message across. It's not about me . . . it's letting God do his work through me.

My ultimate Texas date would be: Having dinner and going to Barnes & Noble to sit down and read.

I love Texas because: It's got everything a person needs. It's home. People still wave at me when I drive down the street. Try that in some other state!

"Don't let anything steal your joy!"

—Stran's Favorite Texas Saying

Wrangler

Stran T Smith

His square-jawed, rugged good looks are the first thing you notice about this friendly young cowboy, and rightly so. Hang around awhile, though, and you'll begin to see what really makes this man from Tell, Texas tick.

It isn't his success as a model, even though his image has been a major factor in the successful launch of a new Wrangler Jean Company product line targeted to 18-24 year-old consumers. His face has appeared in every major pictorial in the western industry including *Texas Monthly*, *Western Horseman* and *Cowboys and Indians*. And it's not his success in the rodeo arena where he has qualified for the last three years at the National Finals Rodeo with the top 15 calf ropers for a World Championship. It isn't even being voted "Fan's Favorite Cowboy" by PRCA fans from across the country or being named one of *People* magazine's "100 Most Eligible Bachelors" for 2000. It's not the line of autograph seekers that appear each time he visits a local western wear retailer. It's not the Harley Davidson or fancy truck you may see him riding through the state of Texas. It's not the money and it's not the fame.

It is, however, his extraordinary ability to balance all of these things and stay true to his beliefs. His deeply rooted faith has been and continues to be an inspiration to many, both young and old.

Stran Smith, good cowboy, good rancher…man of great character. Good for Texas and good for the world. I'm proud to call him my friend.

[signature]

Karl Stressman
Senior Manager of Western Special Events
Wrangler Western Wear

PRINTED ON STOCK MADE FROM RECOVERED DENIM

"…named one of People magazine's '100 Most Eligible Bachelors' for 2000."

I asked Karl Stressman to write my "Tall Texas Tale" because: *He looks better in Wranglers than I do!*

ROY SPENCE
THE IDEA MAN

BUILT A BILLION-DOLLAR AD AGENCY FROM SCRATCH

My Texas post is: President, Gurasich, Spence, Darilek and McClure (GSD&M).

I came into this world on: October 10, 1948 with a headful of ideas!

I was born and raised in: Brownwood, TX— "Deep in the Heart of Texas!"

I hang my hat in: Austin, TX, the city of the forever young.

I'm a real cowboy because: I wear Armani suits & Texas boots!

If you run into my friend Herb Kelleher ask him about the time we: Drank a mayonnaise jar full of Mescal Tequila.

If you walked a mile in my boots: You would know that no one is too good and everyone is good enough.

I love Texas because: We are drillers of everything—oil, ideas & independence!

"Drink up my friends, for tomorrow we ride at dawn!"

—Roy's Favorite Texas Saying

"[GSD&M] coined the slogan 'Texas, It's Like a Whole Other Country.'"

I asked Ann Richards to write my "Tall Texas Tale" because: *She is a Texas epic!*

ANN RICHARDS

July 19, 2000

Dear Martana:

How would I describe Roy Spence? He's part businessman, part evangelist, part visionary and all Texan.

I've known Roy for many years. Back then he ran a small ad agency, but he had a grand dream - that big ideas can generate big results. He wasn't just a dreamer though; he had the moxie to pull it off. He started with five partners and no clients, and he turned that into one of the country's leading agencies. They said that couldn't be done in Texas. New York, Chicago or LA maybe, but not in Texas. Certainly not in Austin.

Roy has a long history of proving people wrong. Like all the folks that thought the 1968 Brownwood Lions football team was too small to be any good. Then a pipsqueak quarterback named Spence led the Lions to a state championship and proved that size isn't everything.

Roy used that same drive and determination to build GSD&M from nothing into a $1 billion company, representing great Texas companies like Southwest Airlines, SBC Communications, Pennzoil and Chili's, and some great not-so Texas companies like Land Rover, Dreamworks and Charles Schwab.

In addition to promoting some of the best companies in the country, Roy and his gang have been great friends of the Lone Star State. For years they promoted Texas tourism, and coined the slogan "Texas, It's Like a Whole Other Country." They launched the Texas Lottery, which provides a great deal of money for state programs. And who can forget "Don't Mess with Texas?" Not only is that one of the most memorable lines in Texas history, but it was the most successful litter prevention campaign in this country's history. A big idea that generated big results. It put GSD&M on the map and made our state a better place.

Some of the biggest names in Texas business count Roy as a friend and advisor - people like Norm Brinker, Herb Kelleher and Red McCombs. He's been a counselor to mayors, congressmen, senators and a couple named Bill and Hillary...and one former governor who is grateful for his friendship and for all the things he's done for the state we both love.

Sincerely,

Ann Richards

ANN W. RICHARDS

P.O. Box 684746 • Austin, Texas 78768-4746

DAVID SQUIRE
DOCTOR OF MONEY

I BLEED ORANGE!

My Texas post is: Financial Advisor, PaineWebber in Dallas, TX.

I came into this world on: August 8, 1969, quickly and loudly.

I hang my hat in: The second-best city—Dallas, TX.

I'm a real cowboy because: I ride the golf range of the Texas fairways with my posse of friends every weekend.

If you run into my friend Bill ask him about the time: I wanted to wash the rental car in Arizona. Think about that one!

If you walked a mile in my boots: You would not take life for granted.

I love Texas because: It's big!

"It never rains on the golf course."

— David's Favorite Texas Saying

"He carefully picks his mentors and follows the teachings of Confucius."

I asked Charles Taylor to write my "Tall Texas Tale" because: *I have known Charles for ten years. In that time we have been business associates, brothers and friends. Regardless, he is one of the greatest people I know and is proving to be a very tough Master!*

ALEXANDER, CHARLES & ASSOCIATES, INC.

CHARLES A. TAYLOR, JR.
CHAIRMAN

13601 PRESTON ROAD, SUITE 211W
DALLAS, TEXAS 75240

September 23, 1999

Dear Martana,

Texas men aren't always just physically big; sometimes they just do big things. When David Squire played football in high school, he made All-District as a 5'8", 158-pound center. David towered over the ball, most of the assistant trainers, and one ref. Yet he was named All-District despite being the smallest interior lineman in Class 5A football. In one sense, that speaks volumes for his big heart.

David typifies "big" in many other ways, too, that do not include machismo. Perhaps the many dashes of cold reality have had a significant influence in David's philosophy of life. He is convinced that life is about choices - just make sure to make the right one! And his choices are made with a mix of empathy and practicality that show wisdom beyond his years. Whether standing by and enduring his wife's serious illness, advising clients and studying the financial markets, or on the golf course, David capitalizes upon his focus and strong character traits built into him by his parents. Well, not always on the golf course. There was that ... but that's not really for here. (Besides, golf sometimes does that to people.)

David's focus brought him from his beloved Austin to Dallas. He thoughtfully researched the opportunities to grow after college, and after careful analysis, disregarded the emotional choice to stay in Austin and returned to his native Dallas to begin his career. None of that is to say that he is averse to returning to Austin many weekends, particularly when UT happens to be playing a football game there.

David is constantly learning, absorbing. His "work hard, play hard" approach to life challenges him to excel at whatever he tackles. He carefully picks his mentors and follows the teachings of Confucius. "The student that does not surpass the Master has failed the Master." And when David surpasses one Master, he picks another and establishes a higher set of goals and standards. Nothing is half-done, rather the complete result of a dedicated effort.

When that great jury in the sky returns the verdict on the selection of real Texas Men, big hearts will reign supreme. Watch this one carefully; he will be on a lot of lists in the future.

Sincerely,

Charles A. Taylor, Jr.

STATE FAIR'S BIG TEX
TEXAS' TALLEST COWBOY

WORLD'S ONLY 52-FOOT TALL
TALKING & WAVING COWBOY!

My Texas post is: Big Texas Circle, where I greet over 3 million visitors a year at the State Fair of Texas in Dallas. I entertain more folks than the President!

I came into this world: Smiling and waving!

I was born and raised in: Born in 1949 in Kerens, TX, where I was originally the world's tallest Santa Claus and transformed into BIG TEX in 1952 by Dallas artist Jack Bridges.

I hang my hat: On my chicken wire and papier-mâché head.

I'm a real cowboy because: My jeans are made of 72 yards of blue denim and weigh in at 65 pounds and . . . my belt buckle is bigger than yours is!

If you run into my friend Jack Bridges (my creator) ask him about the time I: Nearly got blown away during a hurricane in the 50's. The mayor called and yelled at him to tie-me-down because my "waving arm" nearly blew off!

If you walked a mile in my boots: You would be wearing size 70 Dan Post cowboy boots, custom made and podiatrist approved, since I'm on my feet almost four weeks straight every year.

My ultimate Texas date would be: A day of Texas State Fair fun with a real cowgirl. We'd eat Fletcher's corny dogs and funnel cakes, play a few games and then watch the sunset from the highest seat on the Ferris wheel.

I love Texans because: They come back and see me every year.

"Howdy folks! Welcome to the great State Fair of Texas."

— BIG TEX's Favorite Texas Saying

WILLIAMSON-DICKIE MANUFACTURING COMPANY
P.O. BOX 1779 • FORT WORTH, TEXAS 76101
(817) 810-4305 • FAX: (817) 336-5919
pwilliamson@dickies.com

PHILIP C. WILLIAMSON
CHAIRMAN, PRESIDENT
AND
CHIEF EXECUTIVE OFFICER

Dear Martana,

I wanted to share with you a little known fact about the State Fair of Texas' most popular attraction "Big Tex"—he actually started his life as Santa Claus!

Back in 1936, Dallas Mayor "Uncle" Bob Thornton won the Texas Centennial and State Fair for Dallas. Many years later, R. L. Thornton became president of the Sate Fair of Texas and bought the world's tallest Santa Claus from the Kerens, Texas, Chamber of Commerce. He hired Jack Bridges to redesign the over-sized Santa and create Big Tex out of the existing structure.

The original structure was made of chicken wire and papier-mâché. It cost $450 to redesign and redress Santa into Big Tex. Creator Jack Bridges said he modeled Big Tex's facial features after three people: himself, Will Rogers and Doc Simmons (a Texas rancher from Bell County).

Big Tex, all 52 feet of him, has been a sensation ever since his transformation, drawing smiles from nearly three million people annually as he welcomes them with a "Howdy folks!" every year at the State Fair of Texas in Dallas.

As president of Williamson-Dickie, Fort Worth based work clothes manufacturer, I take a lot of pride in the garments we make for Big Tex. Tex's red, white and blue cowboy shirt is the largest we have ever made—it's size 100! Fitting him for his 284-inch waist and 185-inch length jeans isn't an easy task either, but it's an honor to be a part of a Texas tradition.

In 1997, Big Tex received a little cosmetic surgery, "a nip and tuck" as they say, to keep up appearances for the public. His welcome is as warm today as it was over five decades ago, still charming children and adults alike.

But for all of the height, weight and fame, Big Tex is still surprisingly humble and down-to-earth. He's one Texas Man who has a good head on his shoulders, and his feet firmly planted on the fairgrounds. What an honor it is to write a "Tall Texas Tale" for the "Tallest Texas Man" you'll ever meet!

Sincerely,

Philip C Williamson

Philip C. Williamson

I asked Philip Williamson to write my "Tall Texas Tale" because: *Williamson-Dickie of Fort Worth, Texas is the best clothier around. Who else would make my custom size 100 180/181 shirt and my western cut 284W/185L jeans and not complain a stitch?*

" . . . 'BIG TEX' . . . actually started his life as Santa Claus!"

Dickies

RED STEAGALL
OFFICIAL COWBOY POET OF TEXAS

Baxter Black, Head Cowboy • P. O. Box 2190 Benson, Arizona 85602 • (520) 586-1077

November 29, 1999

Dear Martana,

Somewhere in the early eighties I was workin' for a veterinary company and doin' a lot of traveling for them. I was passin' through Fort Worth and went by to see Red. He was packin' up for a trip. Red, who I had just met the year before (which is another story) said, "Why don't you just ride with me down to Schroeder?" "Where's that?" I asked. He said, "Between Austin and San Antonio. You can ride in my new Cadillac with me." "Cool," said I, and we loaded up. He and his band were playin' a dance at Schroeder Hall. I arranged for a friend from Sabinal to meet me at the dance and haul me afterwards to the airport in San Antonio.

As Red and I arrived in the dusty parkin' lot outside the dance hall he said, "Bax, would you do me a favor?" I said, "Sure Red." He was developing into a hero of mine and I would have crawled through twenty-six acres of broken glass just to kiss the dog that did Red's dishes. He handed me a ring of keys that was bigger than a gorilla's hairball and asked, "Would you mind keeping these while I'm onstage? They make such a bulge in my pocket." "Of course, Red," I said. "Anything I can do to help." He walked on in the dance hall and I thought, 'I don't really want to be packin' around two metric tons of keys either.' So I peeled off the Cadillac key and locked the car, and

The dance was magnificent, Red was spectacular, my friend showed up with his date, and the evening wound down. About 12:30 I went and said good-bye to Red and all the band, thanked him with sincere profuseness and headed to his car to retrieve my hanging bag. I inserted the key in the trunk, but it wouldn't turn. I tried it in the door... both of 'em. They were turnless. I began to remember something about General Motors' cars. They had a square key and a round key. One for the ignition, one for the doors. I had the square key. In a panic I tried coat hangers, pocketknives, screwdrivers, magnets, spoon bending, and incantations....all to no avail.

At 1:30 a.m. Red and his band polished off the last set and came out in the parking lot where I was humbly waiting. I offered my explanation blaming General Motors, the science of metallurgy, coat hanger manufacturers and the lack of good car thieves when you needed one. Red was not exactly unpleasant, but he did not think my joke about the guy who locked himself out of the car was funny. "Maybe we could get a locksmith," I suggested feebly. At 2 a.m. Saturday night in Schroeder, Texas the nearest locksmith is in Victoria. He arrived before dawn and quickly did his deed.

"Red," I offered, "I really think I should pay for the locksmith." "Okay," was all he said. I have been a close friend of Red's since those days, although he has never asked me to pack his car keys again.

Sincerely,

baxter black

Baxter Black

> **" . . . I would have crawled through twenty-six acres of broken glass just to kiss the dog that did Red's dishes."**

I asked Baxter Black to write my "Tall Texas Tale" because: *He knows more "Tall Tales" on me than anyone else!*

Honorary Member of The Cowboy Artists of America & Most Beloved Cowboy

My Texas post is: In 43 states with the "Cowboy Corner" radio show and on my Hondo Canyon Ranch.

I came into this world on: December 22, 1938—listening to a story.

I was born & raised in: Born in Gainesville and raised in Sanford, TX.

I hang my hat in: Parker County, ten miles outside Weatherford, TX.

I'm a real cowboy because: I'm not a real cowboy, I just dream of being one.

If you run into my friend Bum Phillips ask him about the time I: Went to the Oilers training camp and how much fun we had singin' cowboy songs all night long!

If you walked a mile in my boots: You'd meet the most wonderful people in the world—my friends.

I love Texas because: Of its heritage, tradition and values.

"I've stayed in California awhile & I've stayed in Tennessee awhile, but the only place I've ever lived is Texas."

— Red's Favorite Texas Saying

JUSTIN LEE STEWART
FIVE-ALARM FIREMAN

"... one of the women on the scene suddenly turned to Justin and said, 'Hey ... it's the Jockey underwear model!!'"

I asked Chief Anderson to write my "Tall Texas Tale" because:

He was "Fireman of the Year" for several years, and he was one of the charter members of the Grapevine Fire Department. He's a mentor to a lot of firefighters.

Grapevine Fire Department

GRAPEVINE
TEXAS

601 Boyd Drive
Grapevine, Texas 76051

Metro 817 410-8100
Fax 817 410-8106

Dear Martana:

Justin Stewart was a simple fireman one day...and a national icon the next!

Let me explain. I hired Justin back in December of '96 to work as a Fire Fighter for the City of Grapevine. He was just a country kid then, who wanted more than anything to save lives. He trained extensively at the Fire Academy in Kilgore, TX, where he got used to living and working in a fire station. He sent out his applications and tested with 22 cities to see if he could get an appointment with them--and after testing in 22 cities, his grades went from 50 to 100 (a perfect score)! He was offered 3 or 4 good jobs, and after a stint in Temple, TX he decided that his home of Grapevine would be the best place to work.

One day his fire station buddies saw a letter that Jockey had sent out, saying that Jockey was looking for some fire fighters to model in a national underwear ad. His friends all said Justin would be the guy who would most likely be chosen, so they rallied him and made Justin go try out.

Sure enough, Justin was picked and flown to NY for the photo shoot, which was printed in magazines across the U.S.A. Shortly after, we had girls from all over calling and asking for the "JOCKEY AD FIREMAN"--and we knew from that point on Justin's life would never quite be the same. Imagine a fireman posing with his trousers down, showing off his skivvies!

Probably the funniest thing happened when Justin went out for an emergency ambulance call. He was dispatched to a call because a child was locked in a car--he responded and helped the mother unlock the car, and rescue the child inside. After all was said and done, one of the women on the scene suddenly turned to Justin and said, "Hey...it's the Jockey underwear model!!" Justin just smiled kind of humbly, tipped his hat, hopped back into the ambulance and went off to his next call.

Justin is a superb fire fighter, trusted member of his EMS team, and a respected friend.

All I can say is that after this book comes out, I just hope the women understand that 911 is for emergency calls only...and not a way to get Justin on the phone!

Sincerely,

Chief David Anderson

Featured Fireman in National Jockey Underwear Ad!

My Texas post is: City of Grapevine Fire Department, Station 4.

I came into this world on: November 24, 1973—puttin' out fires!

I hang my hat in: Grapevine, TX, and my helmet at the fire station.

I'm a real cowboy because: I like to help people when they really need me—when you dial 911, I'm there.

If you run into Division Fire Chief Mark Ashmead ask him about the time we: Had to fight an intense house fire. Smoke filled the house, and we were on our hands and knees crawling to the kitchen. Flames were rolling up the walls . . . and we were just in awe. All we could do was stare. We were amazed by the colors. After 10 seconds, my captain finally said, "We can't just look at this all day—let's put it out now, Stewie."

If you walked a mile in my "fire-resistant" boots: You'd be covered in soot, your hair would get singed and you'd be crawlin' and walkin' over many a hot coal.

My ultimate Texas date would be: A hot air balloon ride with a beautiful woman and a bottle of champagne—soaring over the lights of Dallas.

I love Texas because: I get to rescue beautiful women!

"Dance with the one who brung ya!"

—Justin's Favorite Texas Saying

GEORGE STRAIT

KING OF COUNTRY

24 Albums Certified Gold, Platinum & Multi-Platinum

My Texas post is on: Stages all across Texas and the U.S.A.

I came into this world on: May 18, 1952.

I was born & raised in: Born in Poteet and raised in Pearsall, TX.

I hang my hat in: South Texas mesquite trees, black brush thickets and prickly pear flats.

I'm a real cowboy because: That's the lifestyle I live and enjoy.

If you run into my friend Roy Cooper ask him about the time: I beat him in a horse race in Ruidoso, NM at the All American Futurity.

If you walked a mile in my boots: You would have seen many places and met a lot a great people.

I love Texas because: It's "The Great State."

"You've got to have an Ace in the Hole!"

—George's Favorite Texas Saying

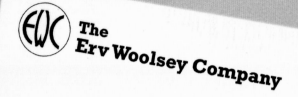

The Erv Woolsey Company

From his background in agriculture and his love of Team Roping, to his Resistol hat, starched jeans, and trademark ropers, fans from all over the world think of George Strait as the symbol of the "Real Texas Man".

While we both graduated from Southwest Texas State University, I met George in 1977 when he and his "Ace in the Hole Band" played my Prairie Rose Nightclub in San Marcos, Texas. I first began to appreciate his music, but very quickly came to appreciate the man, as we became good friends. In the time since, and with far less fanfare than anyone could have imagined, he quietly pieced together one of the most successful careers in the history of the country music business. He did so without a huge ego, while raising a family and keeping his feet planted firmly on the ground. Along the way, he conducted himself in manner and style that has become the standard by which many others will be judged. His loyalty to his friends and staff are legendary, while his quiet confidence, firm handshake and polite manners are the very essence of the real Texas man.

While George is a quiet and very modest person, he also possesses a very warm personality and a tremendous sense of humor. He is a very funny guy who has the ability to use looks and nuances to bring laughter in abundance. His easy going style and ever present smile keeps everyone loose and relaxed.

If we had a dictionary with a definition of the "Real Texas Man", we would instead find a photo of George Strait. I am truly happy to call him my friend.

Sincerely,

Erv Woolsey

Erv Woolsey

1000 18th Avenue South • Nashville, Tennessee 37212
(615) 329-2402 • Fax (615) 327-4917
ewoolsey@telalink.net

"... I met George in 1977 when he and his 'Ace in the Hole Band' played my Prairie Rose Nightclub in San Marcos, Texas."

I asked Erv Woolsey to write my "Tall Texas Tale" because:
He's been a great friend for more than 20 years and he's been with me throughout my career.

HUNTER SULLIVAN
REAL TIME SOUNDTRACK ARTIST

CROONER TO THE STARS!

My Texas post is: President, Search Group Records and DeMers Music Publishing, International.

I came into this world on: August 11, 1965— same as Julius Caesar. I've loved Italian food ever since.

I was born & raised in: Dallas, TX—where I try to stay off Central Expressway and south of Mockingbird Lane!

I hang my hat in: Dallas, TX—singing live in nightclubs all over the planet. I also hang many types of hats in front of the camera performing as an actor.

I'm a real cowboy because: I was raised around them and I love the fact that I am equally comfortable in my boots as I am in a tux. (But I never wear them together!)

If you run into my friend Ron Corcoran ask him about the time I: Cut off all my hair and then got a check in the mail for $1,000.

If you walked a mile in my boots: I'd be barefoot and a mile away.

I love Texas because: It's not Cincinnati!

"Don't write checks with your mouth that your ass can't cash."

—Hunter's Favorite Texas Saying

"(*) # @ %"
Ouch Magazine

Dear Martana,

We have a saying here in Texas ...well, now that I think about it, we have a lot of sayings here in Texas, don't we? Anyway, we like to say that "The Lord never closes one door without opening another." Hopefully, after sharing with you what I consider to be a very "Tall Tale" about one of Texas' brightest, young stars--Hunter Sullivan--you'll see that us Texans was right 'agin!

My grandmother, God rest her soul, used to be one of Hunter's biggest fans. Before she contracted the cancer that would ultimately claim her life, she and I would go see Hunter play, do a little dancing, and maybe have a drink or two. Unfortunately, as her illness progressed, that became impossible for us to do. But that didn't stop Hunter from calling her up to see how she was doing or from stopping by my parents place because "he was in the area." (The area, by the way, is in Southlake--a good, forty minute drive from Dallas).

One day Gramma asked me if I thought Hunter would mind singing a couple of songs at her funeral. "He has such a lovely voice," she said. "Do you think he would charge us much?" Well, I don't mind telling you, Martana, it'd been a long while since I had a laugh that powerful, so I took my own dang time gettin'over it. Everybody knows that Hunter's a shrewd businessman, but for the love of Pete! Besides, he and I had already discussed the matter. Of course, he wouldn't mind. (To tell you the truth, I never even had to ask).

Later, when she was close to the end of her long, arduous fight, Hunter came out to the ranch to discuss the music that he was going to sing at the funeral. He came into Gramma's bedroom, sat down between my Aunt Jean and me, and took my grandmother by her hand and said, "Mildred, the songs you've chosen sure are beautiful. Would you mind if I also performed a hymn that I sang at my grandfather's funeral for you?" She looked at me in surprise and excitement. "Well, Hunter," she asked, "what song is it?" "It's called, 'He Touched Me'," he replied. This was news to me. "How does it go?" I asked. "Well, let's see..." Hunter said, looking upwards and to the left. Then he began to sing. "Shackled by a heavy burden/Need the Lord again and shame/Then the hand of Jesus touched me/And now I am no longer the same." As Hunter's voice grew sturdier with the recollection of the lyrics, my grandmother and aunt began to sing along. "For He touched me/He touched me," they sang, "He touched me and made me whole!"

Suddenly, the most beautiful thing happened. For one, brief, tender, moment, there was no illness...no sadness. Just the three of them locked into one--their voices booming down the halls and into the living room--shocking my family so much that they literally ran into the room to join the chorus.

We have another saying here in Texas. "Character is what you have when no one is looking." Well, I was looking. Hunter Sullivan is definitely a man of character and one hell of a swing performer. I'm proud to be considered a friend of his. (Even though he 'otta know better than to woo the ladies at a time like that!).

All the Best,

David G. Rudduck
Minister of Camaraderie
Ouch! Magazine

4949 Beeman Dallas, Tx. 75226

"One day Gramma asked me if I thought Hunter would mind singing a couple of songs at her funeral."

I asked David Rudduck to write my "Tall Texas Tale" because: *To know him is to love him and because he cracks me up.*

KENNY TROUTT
EXCEL COMMUNICATIONS REVOLUTIONARY

BUILT A BILLION-DOLLAR OUTFIT FASTER THAN ANY OTHER IN U.S. HISTORY!

My Texas post is: Dallas, TX.

I came into this world on: January 8, 1948—on a stream of light fiber.

I hang my hat in: Dallas, TX and Lexington, KY, where I own a horse farm.

I'm a real cowboy because: I own a remuda of fine thoroughbred horses.

If you run into my friend Pete Wittman ask him about the time: Ross Perot came over to welcome me to the neighborhood. Not your average neighbor to "drop by."

If you walked a mile in my boots: You'd work like you don't need the money, love like you've never been hurt and dance like there's nobody lookin'!

I love Texas because: It's still the land of boundless opportunity.

"Winners find ways to win— Losers find excuses."

— Kenny's Favorite Texas Saying

"Once in the very early days when funds were short, Kenny sent $500 to his friend Pete Wittmann to bet on a horse. . . . The horse won. . . . Payroll was met . . ."

I asked Bill Casner to write my "Tall Texas Tale" because: *As a native Texan, he understands my "Texas Spirit"—and he sits a horse real well.*

B&R EQUIPMENT

B & R EQUIPMENT COMPANY, INC.
ADMINISTRATION / OPERATIONS

3100 KELLER HICKS RD • KELLER, TX 76248
OFFICE 817-379-1340 • 214-384-3510 MOBILE
FAX 817-379-2734 • 888-976-4369 TOLL FREE PAGER

As legend has it, Sam Houston came to Texas after a reoccurring dream convinced him that it was his destiny. He crossed the Red River riding a Tennessee mare and bringing with him the confidence and will that would lead an untamed frontier into statehood.

One hundred and fifty years later, another TEXAN to be, Kenny Troutt, would be compelled by his own dream to "pack his tack" and head to the Lone Star State. Texas business and thousands of its citizens would ultimately benefit from those dreams.

I met Kenny in Omaha, Nebraska in 1974. We had both put in a claim for a racehorse named Great Bear Lake. He was an old class horse that had run in "The Derby" and had been previously owned by another Texan named Nelson Bunker Hunt. Claiming is a way of creating parity in racing. If you enter a horse in a claiming race, he is for sale if someone chooses to drop a "claim". In the second "luckiest day in my life" (the first when I met my wife Susan) I won the draw for the claim and got the horse. The rest of my life would be guided by that moment, because that was the day I met Kenny Troutt. Three months later I was training racehorses for Kenny and we would become lifelong friends and business partners. We were both 26 years old, but Kenny was already a major business success and his vision and mental energy amazed me.

Six years later with a wife and the future of two baby girls to consider, I left the nomadic life of the racetrack and returned to my home state of Texas. Kenny and I kept in contact and two years later after having those reoccurring dreams, he sold his business and moved to Texas.

Kenny had always loved the romance of "oil" and after interning with a company for six months, he founded SunTex Resources. Kenny quickly learned the business and acquired some nice leases that produced many productive wells. Business was booming for two years and then oil dropped to $9.00 a barrel. After hanging on for another year, the doors were closed.

Kenny personifies the TEXAS entrepreneurial business spirit. Adversity creates strength; doors that are closed can be reopened to bigger triumphs. The closure of SunTex led to one of the most phenomenal business successes in the history of the U.S.A.

Kenny went on to create Excel Communications, Inc., a telecommunications giant that today is among the largest long distance phone companies in the U. S. Excel became a billion-dollar corporation in eight years, quicker than any company in U.S. history. It was the youngest company to ever be admitted to the New York Stock Exchange and achieved this without borrowing a dime and with a small amount of initial capital provided by himself and three believing friends, Dan, Pete and myself.

It was never easy. The doors could have been closed a thousand times. The weekly question was always "how will payroll be met?" Once in the very early days when funds were short, Kenny sent $500 to his friend Pete Wittmann to bet on a horse running at Oaklawn Park in Arkansas. The horse won and returned $6800 for the bet. Payroll was met and always would be. He always found ways to solve problems that looked insurmountable. Along the way the corner was turned, and Excel became one of the states largest employers and taxpayers. It also became a vehicle for thousands of independent representatives to change their lives.

Excel continues to grow. It thrives under a man that possesses the leadership of Sam Houston, the vision of Stephen F. Austin and the will and negotiating skills of Jim Bowie.

Kenny Troutt – a TEXAS MAN if there ever was one!

Bill Casner

Bill Casner, President
B & R Equipment

JIM TURNER
A TEXAS ORIGINAL

SOLD OVER A BILLION BOTTLES OF DR PEPPER!

My Texas post is: The Dr Pepper/7Up Bottling Group.

I came into this world on: December 18, 1945—with Dr Pepper in my bottle!

I was born & raised in: Houston, TX—where I was allowed only one soft drink a week—can you guess what I picked?

I hang my hat in: Dallas, TX—Dr Pepper capital of the world! Hey, we don't even need taste tests!

I'm a real cowboy because: We support Texas charities every sip of the way!

If you run into my friend Andy ask him about the time I: Scored 63 points in a basketball game in Waco.

If you walked a mile in my boots: You'd appreciate how much work it takes to keep Dr Pepper one of America's top soft drink choices. It's a Cold Cola War out there!

I love Texas because: The people of Texas have supported our products and remained loyal to Dr Pepper. It's because of Texas, the world tastes better!

"When the eagles are silent, the parrots begin to jabber."

—Jim's Favorite Texas Saying

"After college, Jim considered the possibility of playing professional basketball."

I asked Andy Wimpee to write my "Tall Texas Tale" because:

He's a huge Dr Pepper drinker and he knows all my secrets—all but the secret formula for Dr Pepper!

WIMPEE & ASSOCIATES

Dear Martana:

It is my pleasure to have known Jim Turner for 36 years and it is an honor to submit this "Tall Texas Tale". He has been a successful "Tall Texan" from his high school days at Sam Houston, his college days at Baylor University, his business career with both Dr Pepper Bottling Company of Texas, and currently as CEO of the Dr Pepper/Seven Up Bottling Group, Inc.

I have known Jim since we were both 18 and freshmen at Baylor University. While at Baylor, Jim had a passion for sports, namely basketball. He became an all Southwest Conference player and inducted in the Baylor Sports Hall of Fame. In particular, I can remember one game in 1964 when he scored 63 points. This was a remarkable feat because it was long before the 3 point conversion. There was never any question, that when Jim crossed mid-court he was ready to jump, shoot and score. He had such a drive and determination to succeed even then. During this time, Jim was my fraternity big brother and I can remember telling him "when I grow up I want to be just like you."

After college, Jim considered the possibility of playing professional basketball. Instead, he made a choice to go into the business world and began a career in the soft drink industry. Within a very short time, he became a leader in the industry and in 1997 became the largest soft drink bottler in the United States. When I called him to congratulate him, his comment was "it was a team effort and we did it together." I said to Jim, "some people make things happen, some people watch things happen, and some people wonder what happened, you make things happen. When I grow up I still want to be just like you." Further exemplifying his accomplishments over the years, Jim received the prestigious Horatio Alger Award in 1998.

Not only is Jim an outstanding leader in the business world, but he is a compassionate humanitarian. Along with his wife, Julie, they are actively involved in over 20 diverse community and charitable activities. Since 1968 when I was in their wedding, I have known Jim and Julie to be a strong and compassionate couple. Together, they are advocates for many educational and youth programs. Their total commitment and caring for others has been a strong positive reinforcement to many including my family. Their loving and caring spirit is evident through their two beautiful daughters, Amy and Jenna.

My friend, Jim Turner, continues to make his mark whether he is involved in business, or community activities, or hitting a drive of 300 yards, or sinking that 3-foot putt. He is a "Tall Texan" both in stature and in spirit. Texas will certainly continue to benefit from his contributions.

Sincerely,

Andy Wimpee

Andy Wimpee

5205 Old Shepard • Plano, Texas 75093 • 972-248-8227

GARY TYLOCK, M.D.
OPTHAMOLOGIST & LASIK VISION SURGEON

> "Later that morning while meeting with Dr. Tylock he happily informed me that I was 20/20!"

I asked George Dunham to write my "Tall Texas Tale" because: *His eyes sing to the rhythm of Texas music!*

Dear Martana:

A couple of years ago I was one of the most unlikely candidates to have LASIK eye surgery. As a radio personality I was approached by several centers to have the procedures in exchange for being a spokesman for their practice. I turned down several opportunities because I didn't feel comfortable with the idea of having surgery on my eyes. I couldn't even deal with using contact lenses. I had been a long time glasses wearer and just looked at it as necessary. I had accepted the fact that I would wear glasses for the rest of my life, that is until I met Dr Gary Tylock and his staff.

I went to their office with the full intent of telling them "thanks but no thanks" when it came to getting the LASIK procedure. However, after meeting Dr Tylock, seeing his caring and easy going style and studying his accomplishments and success, I was convinced that LASIK surgery would be worth looking into. I noticed that every one I spoke with had nothing but great things to say about Dr Tylock and how he had orchestrated a change in their life.

Throughout the entire process Dr Tylock made sure that I was comfortable and treated with the utmost respect. And yes, they were right: it does make all the difference in the world. I was able to return to work early the next morning with out glasses for the first time in my life. Later that morning while meeting with Dr Tylock he happily informed me that I was 20/20!

From calling games for the University of North Texas, to seeing highway signs, my vision is now incredible. I no longer have to worry about my glasses fogging up or breaking in a game of pickup basketball.

My life has been changed thanks to the outstanding work of "Texas Man" Gary R. Tylock, MD and his staff. I truly Have a new vision for my life!

Sincerely,

George Dunham

SPORTSRADIO STATION OF THE YEAR!

ALL SPORTS. ALL THE TIME.

3500 Maple Avenue • Suite 1310 • Dallas TX, 75219
214.526.7400 • Fax 214.525.2525 • Sales Fax 214.525.2545 • www.theticket.com

PERFORMED OVER 20,000 VISION CORRECTION PROCEDURES SINCE 1986

My Texas post is: My office and Laser Suite located about four miles west of Texas Stadium in Irving, TX.

I came into this world on: A starry night on April 19, 1952.

I hang my hat in: Las Colinas, overlooking the golf course.

I'm a real cowboy because: The laser I shoot is a match for any gun in the West.

If you run into my friends ask them about: My computerized CD music collection. It's a computerized 800 CD juke box that can do everything but cook! This is the best way to organize a music library and have it all at your fingertips.

If you walked a mile in my boots: You'd see a lot of patients smile and you might notice eyes in your dreams.

My ultimate Texas date would be: A long weekend visiting San Francisco and surrounding areas. We would tour the countryside including the wine country. In the city we would visit some of the art galleries and different shops. Other activities may include a boat ride to Sausalito or a helicopter ride over the Bay. A walk in the Botanical Gardens or on the beach at sunset is always enjoyable. At night we would dine and dance in some of the best restaurants overlooking the picturesque San Francisco Bay.

I love Texas because: Of its people and mild winters.

"If it's not broken, don't fix it. Unless it's an upgrade."

— Gary's Favorite Texas Saying

BRIAN VASSALLO
IL COWBOY ITALIANO

I'M STILL ALIVE!

My Texas post is: Founder, Automotive Resource Group—a leading supplier of automotive insurance and aftermarket products.

I came into this world on: November 25, 1956—late for a tee time!

I was born & raised in: Dallas, TX, on my mama's lasagna.

I hang my hat in: Dallas and on the highways and golf courses all over Texas.

I'm a real cowboy because: After six years in New York City, there's no place like home!

If you run into my friend Jason Fisher ask him why: My friends in New York City called me the Cartier Cowboy.

If you walked a mile in my boots: You would have been served airline food all across the United States and back!

My ultimate Texas date would be: Floating the canals of Venice on a Gondola, while Pavoritti serenades me and my date.

I love Texas because: The two most important people in my life are Texans—my daughters.

"To hell with it, they can't eat you!"

—Brian's Favorite Texas Saying

"Brian Vassallo breezed [in] on a cloud of cologne, wearing a silk shirt, bellbottoms and platform shoes."

I asked Greg Hunt to write my "Tall Texas Tale" because: *We were college running buddies and roommates. He was a cowboy from Lubbock and had never met someone so foreign lookin' before.*

G & H MANUFACTURING, Ltd.
1015 COMMERCIAL BLVD. S. · ARLINGTON, TX 76001
OFFICE: (817) 467-9883 · FAX (817) 468-3272
ACCOUNTING: FAX (817) 477-4922

Dear Martana:

Brian Vassallo breezed into the FIJI Lodge at Texas Tech University in 1975 on a cloud of cologne, wearing a silk shirt, bellbottoms and platform shoes. We West Texas cowboys wondered first, "What the blankety blank is that?" and second, "How many fights are we going to have to defend him in?" One idiot even tried to blackball him because he was "too Italian." We learned very quickly that underneath all that flash was a big-hearted, generous, true-blue friend who would be there when the chips were down and make it all fun and interesting in the process.

I have never met a more loyal or supportive friend, or anyone with more energy and drive. Brian works hard, plays hard and never seems to tire of either. He's a successful entrepreneur who owns an agency that sells ancillary services for the automotive industry, an avid golfer, hunter, fisherman and the father of two beautiful University of Texas coeds. The Italian in him loves great food and good times, but it's the Texan in him that makes him such a good businessman, friend and father.

My history with Brian goes through many chapters: college life, marriage and children, divorce and dating, business successes and failures; but throughout those 25 years, he's consistently been a solid friend and supportive father. He loves his daughters, and they factor heavily in everything he does and every choice he makes. My wife adores him because he looks a woman in the eye and talks to her and laughs with her without any "weird undercurrents." The ladies appreciate Brian--not because he's a Casanova, but because he likes women as people. He cares about them, genuinely listens to them, respects their opinions, and like all Italians--he truly enjoys their company.

The key to Brian and his appeal is very simple: family. He comes from a big, close "Texas-Italian" family who all enjoy life to the fullest. They're still tight no matter what befalls them or where they are scattered across the country. He transfers that generosity and charisma to all who truly know him and to some who have never met him. Along with other charitable contributions, he once donated a car to a woman who needed transportation to and from the doctor for a child who was awaiting a kidney transplant.

Wherever we have lived and no matter how much time has gone by, I know he's still a friend I can count on for anything, and that's a rarity. I believe Brian embodies all that makes Texans great--lust for life, loyalty, courage and a true independent spirit!

Sincerely,

Greg M. Hunt
President and Managing Partner

JIMMIE HAGGAR VAUGHAN
RANCHER & RODEO COWBOY

"When Jimmie is not 'punchin' doggies' on the JHV Ranch or at rodeos from Texas to Wyoming . . ."

I asked Michael Allen McBee to write my "Tall Texas Tale" because: *We've been friends for 20 years. Growing up we shared a lot of experiences together. We've been friends through a lot—good times and bad, but he still doesn't trust me enough to get in an airplane when I'm flying!*

McBEE OPERATING COMPANY, L.L.C.
3738 OAK LAWN, LB 200
DALLAS, TEXAS 75219
(214) 526-1500 • FAX (214) 521-6335

February 2, 2000

Dear Martana,

From his youngest days, this grandson of clothing magnate J. M. Haggar has been an equestrian of Texan proportions. Childhood paint ponies gave way to hunter jumpers, then award winning polo matches and championship rodeos. Throughout his years, James Haggar Vaughan has ridden his way across Texas and beyond. Born and raised in Dallas, Jimmie now splits his time between his hill country ranches, rodeos and high adventure. His mother Rosemary Haggar Vaughan chairs the philanthropic Haggar Foundation, well known and greatly appreciated in Dallas for it's generous contributions to a number of worthy causes.

When Jimmie is not "punchin' doggies" on the JHV Ranch or at rodeos from Texas to Wyoming, he may be found in black tie and boots at his mother's side, or in Wranglers and waders fishing with his father Ed Vaughan up at his fishing lodge in Alaska. This one time PRCA Rookie of the Year cowboy is equally at ease in the saddle chasing steers as he is chasing a polo ball with his good friend and neighbor actor Tommy Lee Jones. Always camera friendly, Jimmie may add to his modeling portfolio from time to time or as of most recent, be found in the New Mexico desert with another good friend and actor Brad Johnson hunting trophy mule deer with a TV outdoorsman show.

As a best friend of more than twenty years, I am uniquely qualified to tell a Texas Tale on Jimmie. Forgoing a tally of tales most would think taller than true, we'll go back with Jimmie to the simpler days when an innocent boy full of Saturday westerns and decked out as a little Randolph Scott rides his paint pony through the wild, wild ranges of Strait Lane in Dallas. Padding through the trees on his trusty steed, Jimmie spies equally little Tammy McCutchin from next door riding her pony. Out from the trees, Jimmie ambushes the rear of Tammy's pony with his trusty Red Rider BB gun. In short order, Tammy was afoot and Jimmie was moving ever closer to having his rear engaged by his father. We all know that the formidable Red Rider BB gun "can shoot your eye out", as an addendum, we can note they play havoc on ponies too. Well, Tammy got back into the saddle again and she remained friends with that young cowpoke. Jimmie swears up and down that he hasn't shot the horse out from under a good looking girl ever since.

Michael A. McBee, Jr.

Pro-Rodeo Cowboy Association Rookie of the Year, 1995

My Texas post is: Owner of the J.H.V. Ranch in Fredonia, TX, where we raise premium stocker and feeder calves.

I came into this world on: February 6, 1962—buckin'.

I was born & raised in: Dallas, TX with my brother and three sisters.

I hang my hat in: Fredonia, TX—in the center of the beautiful Hill Country.

I'm a real cowboy because: That is definitely not bean-dip on the bottom of my cowboy boots!

If you run into my friend Brad Johnson ask him about: How he pinned the name Chief Broken Foot on me at the Pendleton Round-up Rodeo in Oregon. Yes, my foot was actually broken, and no it didn't happen in the rodeo!

If you walked a mile in my boots: You'd have blisters on your feet.

My ultimate Texas date would be: To saddle up two horses, ride through the La Bamba Pasture on the ranch to the highest point and have a picnic under a windmill on top of the hill.

I love Texas because: Of the wide open spaces.

Rope 'em when they up, tie 'em when they down."

— Jimmie's Favorite Texas Saying

J. CESAR VIRAMONTES
STONE WASH SWASHBUCKLER

" . . . he prefers to ride his Harley Davidson motorcycle making his rounds . . . "

I asked Ted Houghton to write my "Tall Texas Tale" because: *He is a good friend and I feel our friendship was inherited from his late father. Ted is also an avid supporter of our community as well as educational causes, so that alone is a common denominator between us.*

ECH IV

Building Relationships • Designing Concepts • Providing Quality Customer Service • Since 1974

Ted Houghton, Jr.
Life Member Million Dollar Round Table

June 5, 2000

Estate Planning Products
Business Insurance
Executive Benefits

Dear Martana:

The Houghton's and Cesar Viramontes go back several decades. The relationship started with my late father. Both Cesar and my father have a genuine love and compassion for people. So it was not surprising to me that they related to one another. As my father consistently reminded me "never forget where you come from" and "remember the people not as fortunate as you", these sayings are what describe Cesar Viramontes.

Cesar credits Levi Strauss & Co. (LS&CO) for his success. He has been doing business with LS&CO since 1984 and is their largest contractor in the United States.

Most comfortable wearing his trademark Levi brand jeans, Cesar can be found in the evenings at any watering hole preferably in the south or Mexican side of El Paso, close to the border drinking Coors, Miller or Tecate, beer products that he distributes as the owner of Montana Beverage Co.

Cesar, who does not take himself serious, is a Texan by choice, having been born on the Mexican side of the border 40 miles from El Paso. As a form of relaxation, he prefers to ride his Harley Davidson motorcycle making his rounds to visit his children and numerous friends.

Over the years Cesar has leveraged his business success to make a difference in his community and in the state of Texas. To highlight a few of Cesar's interests and contributions, he has become involved in helping young people to get an education at the grade school level, high school and at the college level. He sits on the board of the largest locally owned bank and focuses on making loans to the community's businesses to ensure economic growth. Cesar also spends time as Chairman of the Board of Commissioners of the Housing Authority of the City of El Paso, an entity that provides affordable housing to lower income families.

Congressman Silvestre Reyes appointed Cesar to the Congressional Hispanic Caucus Institute, a business forum that gives Hispanics, El Paso and Texas a voice in Washington.

In a nutshell, a lean 6'1, Cesar Viramontes is a well rounded people's man, one that finds himself comfortable rubbing elbows with the elite but even more so in the "barrio" where he comes from, with the people that most make him feel like one of them. Indeed, a True Texas Man.

Sincerely,

Ted Houghton, Jr.

• Agent • Signator Insurance Agency of Texas, Inc., an affiliate of John Hancock Life Insurance Company • Boston, MA •
• Registered Representative • Signator Investors, Inc., Member NASD, SIPC • 124 Castellano, Suite 202 • El Paso, Texas 79912 • 915-544-2940 •

The Commons • 4171 N. Mesa Building A, Suite 102 • El Paso, Texas 79902 • 915 541-7055 • Fax: 915 577-0751

Pioneer & First Provider of Stone Wash Jeans for Levi Strauss & Co.

My Texas post is: CEO, International Garment Processors and Montana Beverage Company in El Paso, TX.

I came into this world: One day after the 4th of July in 1940. My mom says I am still restless today because of those firecrackers.

I was born & raised in: Born in the town of San Ignacio in Chihuahua, Mexico and raised in El Paso—where we are a part of Texas and the USA, but we are 75% Mexican.

I hang my hat in: El Paso, TX, at a watering hole 1/2 mile from the Mexican border. Since I'm a distributor for Coors and Miller beers, it's part of my job to drink it! (Quality control, you know.)

I'm a real cowboy because: I stone wash the jeans the cowboys wear. They wouldn't be so cool if it weren't for the way I wash their jeans. However, I ride a Harley Davidson instead of a horse.

If you run into my friend Gilbert ask him about the time we: Split after a late-night party and decided to drive to California. About half way there we realized it was a much longer drive than expected and came back home.

If you walked a mile in my boots: You would be drinking lots of beer and needing a shoe shine.

I love Texas because: It's the one state were Mexicans have had a great influence in culture, architecture and art—not to mention the food. If it weren't for our Mexican influence, gringos wouldn't be drinking margaritas and eating enchiladas three nights a week!

"You either do things right or you do things wrong. There's nothing in between."

—Cesar's Favorite Texas Saying

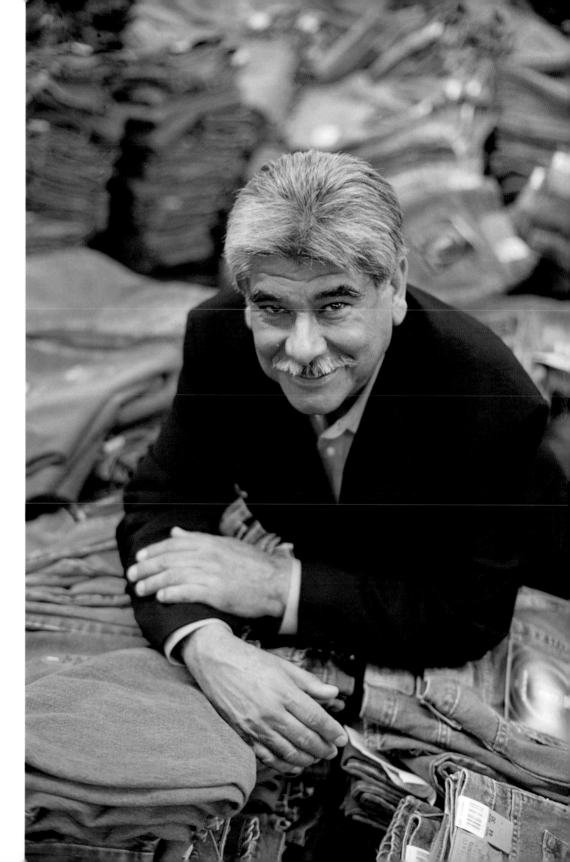

BOB "DADDY-O" WADE
PROFESSIONAL TEXAN-ARTIST AT LARGE

I CAN DO YO-YO TRICKS WHILE RIDING BACKWARDS ON A BICYCLE!

My Texas post is: CEO, Art Director and Head Lackey of PROJECTS & PHOTOWORKS in Austin, TX. I run around the country making giant sculptures, like the 40-ft. iguana on the roof of the Lone Star Cafe in New York City, frogs in Dallas, giant boots in San Antonio and a 70-ft. saxophone in Houston. In my spare time, I airbrush color on giant photo mural enlargements of vintage images like cowgirls and Pancho Villa. They're shown in galleries, museums and T-shirts near you.

I came into this world on: January 6, 1943, "King's Day"—with the help of some wartime forceps.

I was born & raised in: Austin, but lived all over Texas in hotels, as the only child of hotel manager "Chaffin" and wife "Pattie." I spent the most time in El Paso and Juarez.

I hang my hat in: A limestone cool pad in Austin, TX, near the lake, on a cul-de-sac not far from where I was born.

I'm a real cowboy because: I wear an early pair of Larry Mahan boots, drive a pick-up, listen to Kinky, Willie and the boys and . . . I am Roy Rogers' second cousin.

If you run into my friend Monk White ask him about the time: We went to Paris, France, looking for my customized 1947 "Spartan Trailer" (The Texas Mobile Home Museum) that gypsies had stolen after the 1977 Biennale Exhibit. (We found everything BUT the trailer!)

If you walked a mile in my boots: It wouldn't be in New York City (it'll kill your feet), so sometimes I wear Black Converse All-Stars.

I love Texas because: Tex-Mex, barbecue, beer joints, blondes, wheeler-dealers, great characters, friendly people, good humor and BIG everything!

"It's the kind of stuff you like, if you like that kind of stuff."

—Daddy-O's Favorite Texas Saying

COWBOYS&INDIANS

20 July 2000

Martana, My Dear,

A 25-foot-long set of steer horns. A 40-foot-long iguana. A 100-foot-long rattlesnake. Dimensions like these are truly Texan in size, and the only artist capable of manhandling such proportions is himself an iconic Texas figure.

To art aficionados and his intimates, he is the "Daddy-O." The uninitiated call him Mr. Wade. Museum curators and gallery owners list him simply as Robert Schrope Wade. A native Texan (Class of '43) and a graduate of the University of Texas at Austin, the Daddy-O has redefined for his fellow Texans, as well as the unwashed masses who live beyond the borders of the Lone Star State, concepts such as "painting with broad strokes" and "using a big brush."

Two perfect examples of the Daddy-O's larger-than-life vision stand along Loop 410 in the Alamo City. There, by North Star Mall, a pair of custom-crafted cowboy boots tower 40 feet, beckoning shoppers, inviting the curious, and even providing sanctuary for enterprising transients. Yet few realize that in addition to the popular appeal of his oversized works, the Daddy-O is also one of our state's most highly sought after artists.

The Royal Palace of Monaco, the Pompidou Center in Paris, the State Capitol of New Mexico, and the Menil Collection in Houston are only a few of the prestigious addresses where his giant hand-tinted photo works hang. Add private collectors like Robert Redford, Sam Shepard, Glenn Frey, and yours truly, and it is clear that the man will sell his work to just about anyone with a keen eye and good credit.

Martana, I suggest you make your way to www.bobwade.com and see for yourself why the Daddy-O is not only an artist of truly Texas proportions but a natural selection for your distinguished roll.

Happy Trails,

Eric

Eric O'Keefe
Editor

8214 Westchester Drive ★ Suite 800 ★ Dallas, TX 75225
phone (214) 750-8222   fax (214) 750-4522   e-mail cowboysindians.com

"A 25-foot-long set of steer horns. A 40-foot-long iguana. A 100-foot-long rattlesnake."

I asked Eric O'Keefe to write my "Tall Texas Tale" because: *He's a great journalist who knows my act and is at least as bad as me.*

KENT WALDREP
BORN LEADER & CRUSADER

May 22, 2000

To the Texas Men: Big Guns, Rising Stars and Cowboys!

It is a pleasure to submit this "Tall Texas Tale" about Kent Waldrep because Kent's numerous invaluable contributions and achievements continue to inspire us all.

On a personal level it was in 1974 that I first became aware of Kent. He was injured playing football for TCU and it was when I played for the Dallas Cowboys. Those of us involved in sports in the Metroplex were keenly aware of Kent's injury and his early efforts to improve his situation. In fact, Kent and I were together at a Texas Sports Hall of Fame luncheon at the Colonial Country Club in Fort Worth in the spring of 1975 shortly after his injury. As Kent graciously accepted his award that day, I remember his remarks about not giving up hope of walking again. Kent's words ring even louder today because of my most recent involvement in the Tenth Annual Southwestern Ball.

Back in 1989, Kent and Dr. Kern Wildenthal, UT Southwestern Medical School, decided to join forces to build a world-class paralysis research center in Dallas. The major fundraising effort began the next year with a gala chaired by Ron and Sandi Haddock of FINA. This year the Haddocks and my wife, Marianne, and I co-chaired the event to celebrate the culmination of a $10 million fundraising campaign to build the Kent Waldrep Center for Basic Neuroscience Research at UT Southwestern.

It was no surprise to my family when we learned the Waldreps were honored by the Dallas YWCA as the 1998 Family of the Year. To their credit, the Waldreps give of their time and financial resources to the cause of paralysis and serve on many non-profit organizations and state agencies. Kent's public service includes working with three U.S. Presidents where he was instrumental in the inception and drafting of the Americans with Disabilities Act.

A fourth-generation Texan born on Texas Independence Day, Kent continues to leave his mark on our local and national landscape. Respecting and understanding the history of this great award, in my opinion Kent Waldrep is a Texas Man of Excellence!

Best regards,

THE STAUBACH COMPANY

Roger T. Staubach
Chairman and CEO

15601 Dallas Parkway, Suite, 400, Dallas, TX 75001

972.361.5000 (fax 972.361.5912)

> " . . . I remember his remarks about not giving up hope of walking again."

I asked Roger Staubach to write my "Tall Texas Tale" because: *Other than my father, he is the one man who has influenced my life the most.*

Co-Author of the
Americans with Disabilities Act (ADA)

My Texas post is: Clark's barbecue in Tioga, TX—where the meringue on a pie is eight inches high!

I came into this world on: Texas Independence Day, March 2, 1954!

I was born & raised in: Born in Austin, TX in University of Texas' student housing, and raised from El Paso to Grand Prairie to Alvin, TX.

I hang my hat in: Celina, TX, where we pray before we play.

I'm a real cowboy because: I'm a fourth-generation Texan.

If you run into my friend Terry ask her about: Sixth Street, Austin, TX: Doug English, the Lone Star Classic and my butt sticking straight up in the air! Let's just say, I have two left wheels.

If you walked a mile in my boots: Give them back! I want to walk that mile.

I love Texas because: We love God and life, in that order.

"If you ain't the lead dog, the scenery never changes."

—Kent's Favorite Texas Saying

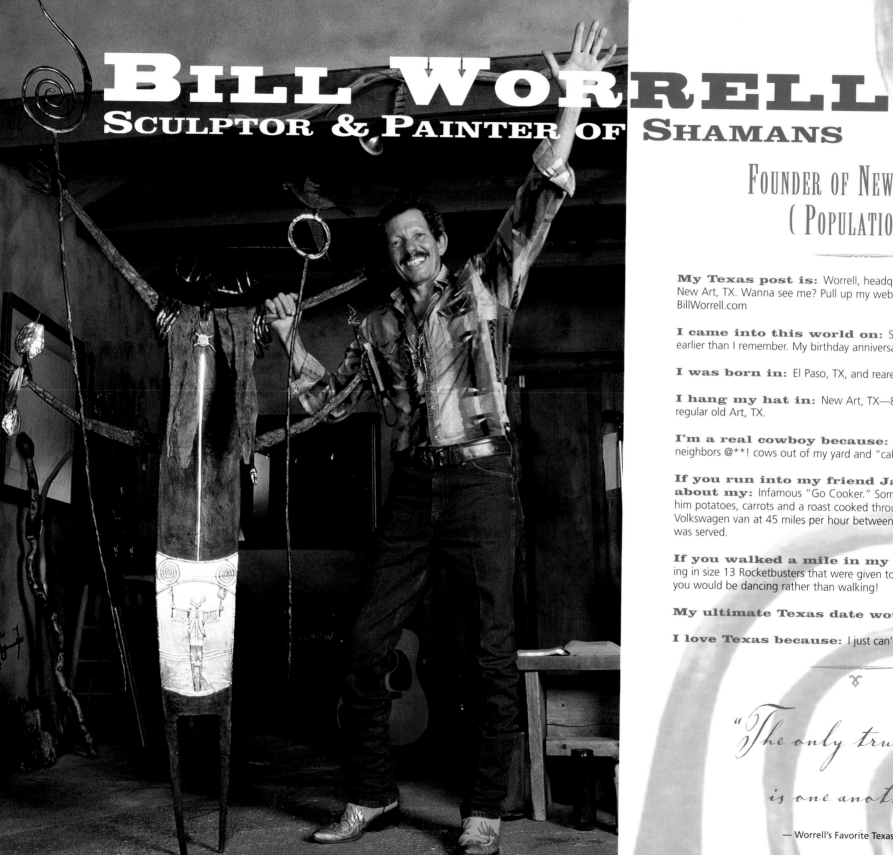

BILL WORRELL
SCULPTOR & PAINTER OF SHAMANS

FOUNDER OF NEW ART, TX
(POPULATION 1)

My Texas post is: Worrell, headquartered on the Llano River in New Art, TX. Wanna see me? Pull up my website at shamanartsinc.com or BillWorrell.com

I came into this world on: September 5, 1935, earlier than I remember. My birthday anniversary is also September 5.

I was born in: El Paso, TX, and reared in Colorado City, TX.

I hang my hat in: New Art, TX—8 miles down the dirt road from regular old Art, TX.

I'm a real cowboy because: Just this morning I chased my neighbors @**! cows out of my yard and "caked" my own cows.

If you run into my friend Jay Adams ask him about my: Infamous "Go Cooker." Sometime around 1971, I served him potatoes, carrots and a roast cooked through the tail pipe of an old Volkswagen van at 45 miles per hour between Odessa and Lubbock. Dinner was served.

If you walked a mile in my boots: You would be walking in size 13 Rocketbusters that were given to me by Kix Brooks. Most likely you would be dancing rather than walking!

My ultimate Texas date would be: Sandra Bullock.

I love Texas because: I just can't help it!

"The only true wealth is one another."

— Worrell's Favorite Texas Saying

"It's called art, but I think it's medicine."

Dear Martana,

The more time I spend on the road the more I look forward to coming home. When I walk through the door I am blessed with a wonderful wife, two great kids, and a home that gives me the peace I need to charge my batteries for the next "go 'round". One of the first things I see is a collection of "shaman" sculptures by Bill Worrell hanging on and standing by a large stone fireplace. What strikes me as so wonderful about these creations, is not just the warmth and spirit that they provide but more importantly the sacred memories and friendship of the man who created them.

I met Bill on the video set for a new song our group Brooks and Dunn had coming out called "'BOOT SCOOT BOOGIE". I had no idea at the time what a wonderful effect this person would have on my life. He was draped in small gold and silver sculptures of little primitive looking figures. Most had what looked like deer heads with antlers and were hanging around his neck on leather strands. There was even a collection on a golden band around his well worn hat. Noone else short of an Aztec priest could have gotten away with this display of precious metal, but on this man it was a natural part of his costume.

Without meeting Worrell it is hard to truly appreciate the warmth of his character, but his art does go a long way towards helping to make the connection. There is a sense of respect in all that he does and where it comes from. He has researched the Indians whose cave drawings have inspired much of his work extensively, and it is apparent he reaches far beyond earthly boundaries for his muse.

Recently I was exploring some land I wanted to buy and came across a cemetery deep in the woods with two hundred year old tombs that were in various states of "exposure". You can guess who I called to find out what I should do. On our Greatest Hits package we list Bill as "Spiritual Guru" and on a road that gets very long sometimes, he is a true oasis for the soul.

God bless Texas for giving us this wonderful man.

Sincerely,

Kix Brooks

P.O. BOX 120669 NASHVILLE, TN 37212

Martana Hanson

June 11, 1998

Dear Martana:

I don't remember where exactly it was that I met Worrell. It seems like he just kind of appeared, much like one of those ghost-like shamans that he works so successfully with. Both are inhabitants of the here and now and the spiritually great, yet highly sought after, unknown.

Originality, in any form is hard to find. In the field of art, it is the most desired yet seldom realized treasure there is. You don't find it, it finds you. And when it does, your world and those that it is shared with becomes a better place.

Although I think his work far exceeds region or title, Bill is recognized as one of the most successful southwest contemporary artists of today.

It all started in a little bitty cave, in a great big state, Texas. What Bill found that day is far better explained by him than me. What it started was a fantastic philosophical journey through spiritualism expressed through sculpture, painting and thought provoking writing.

It's called art, but I think it's medicine. A Texan from his hat down to his boots. I'm a Texan and proud to call him friend.

Ronnie Dunn

- Ronnie Dunn -

900 Division Street • Nashville, Tennessee 37203

I asked Brooks & Dunn to write my "Tall Texas Tale" because:

These guys know how to write music, sing music, boot scoot and appreciate good art. They are philosophers. Who better could I get?

My Favorite Texas Man

Texas Man's "Name"

Texas Man's "Title"

*Place
"My Favorite Texas Man"
Photo Here*

Texas Man's "Claim to Fame"

My Texas post is:

I came into this world on:

I was born and raised in:

I hang my hat in:

I'm a real cowboy because:

If you run into my friend
ask about the time I:

If you walked a mile in my boots:

My ultimate Texas date would be:

I love Texas because:

"

"

– Texas Man's "Favorite Texas Saying"

Place
"Tall Texas Tale"
Letter Here

"

—Favorite "Tall Texas Tale" Quote

I asked _____ to
write my "Tall Texas Tale" because: _____

MARTANA
ENTREPRENEUR, AUTHOR & DIPLOMAT

ROPED TEXAS' TOP BIG GUNS, RISING STARS & COWBOYS & BRANDED THEM WITH THE HONOR OF TEXAS MEN

My Texas post is: The TEXAS MEN office in Dallas, TX, and Partner, Ranch Texas Entertainment, Ltd.

I came into this world on: November 20—a shooting star ready for adventure!

I was born & raised in: Born in Texarkana (on the Texas side of course) and raised in several cities across the Lone Star State.

I hang my hat in: My "treehouse"—overlooking the city lights of the Dallas skyline from high above.

I'm a real cowgirl because: I put *Texas Men* on coffee tables all over the world!

If you run into my friend Bill Worrell ask him about the time I: Attended his Easter Beer Hunt. Bill hid long neck beers and I filled up my "Easter Six Pack" first and won the grand prize—a bouquet of Hill Country wild flowers.

If you walked a mile in my boots: You would have met real characters and beautiful souls.

My ultimate Texas date would be: A surprise! He would pick me up and whisk me off to the nearest airport or heli-pad for an amazing evening of Texas-sized surprises!

I love Texas because: There's nothing more comforting than returning home to a familiar Texas drawl and my grandmother's fried catfish!

"Don't ever ask a Texan where he's from, if he's from Texas he'll tell you —if he's not . . . don't embarrass him!"

— Martana's Favorite Texas Saying

RECIPE FOR A TEXAS MAN

2 pints pure charm

1 cup strong silence

1/2 teaspoon saltiness

1 gallon of honor

4 cups independence

1 honest handshake

2 or 3 great laughs

1 big Southern heart

1 tinge of Texas drawl

a pinch of sunburn
(cover with 10-gallon cowboy hat)

Stir in discipline, pride and integrity. Mix well until character is thoroughly formed.
Combine great looks, unique talents and a good bit of hard-earned money.
Fold in a rich belief in God, country and family. Serves people Worldwide.

-Brooke Malouf

CONTRIBUTORS

Laurel Barrett

Showing true Texas style in her high-bred work with TEXAS MEN, Marketing Director Laurel Barrett traveled high and low across the Lone Star State interviewing TEXAS MEN candidates. These TEXAS MEN provided the ultimate in transportation—private planes, helicopters, Jeeps and horses!

One of Laurel's adventures took her to "new heights" in Alpine, TX, courtesy of Rancher and Cattle Baron Al Micallef. "Martana and I arrived in Al's private plane at the tiny Alpine airstrip when out of the blue Al and a movie star, Brad Johnson, flew in to pick us up via helicopter!" Laurel remembers. "With Hollywood good looks, Johnson stepped out to greet us and then we were whisked away for a tour of Al's ranch, listening to *Out of Africa* while soaring above the canyons." Now that was a Big Texas Welcome!

laurel@2CHARITe.com

Andrea Chestnut

Andrea is a genuine "Georgia Peach"—born and raised. She spent her life living in the Atlanta area until moving to Dallas in 1997. This "ORGANIZING WIZ" has kept the wheels greased and rollin' behind the scenes at Texas Men over this past year. Juggling these strong Texas Men with the dynamic Martana is a daunting task for anyone! Andrea is a fantastic cook. She can whip up anything from a down-home Southern meal to an exquisite cordon bleu dinner. This dynamic lady feels more at home in Dallas than she ever was in her native Atlanta.

Matt Hahn

Our TEXAS MEN crew was scheduled to fly into Santa Barbara, CA from Texas first thing in the morning and wanted to meet for breakfast. Matt's dilemma was to find a restaurant fit for four hungry Texans, one of whom owns one of the largest cattle ranches in Texas. Taking us to an all-organic vegetarian restaurant was out of the question. Matt thought it more appropriate to go to one of the most scenic places in all of California—the Santa Ynez Valley, home to horse and cattle ranches. At the top of the hill, buried under old-growth sycamores and cottonwoods, our crew pulled into an 1800s stagecoach stop turned restaurant—Cold Spring Tavern. Sitting around a table by the fire, we discussed the design aspects of this very book. The atmosphere was perfect for our "California-style Texas breakfast" of steak, eggs, venison chili and pork chops—of course!

Based in Buellton, CA, Matt Hahn, ThinkDesign, has been designing museum-quality books for 13 years to include *Saddlemaker to the Stars* and *Bit and Spur Makers in the Vaquero Tradition*.

Shelly Johnson

The last thing anyone would guess about Pre-Press Expert Shelly Johnson is that she isn't from Texas. With true Texas spirited enthusiasm and expert eyes—Shelly examined hundreds of photos of Texas Men to bring out their true colors.

Shelly also has a passion for cooking, so it wasn't long until she discovered her favorite Texas Man, chef and author Grady Spears. After receiving an autographed copy of his cookbook, *A Cowboy in the Kitchen,* Shelly whipped-up a batch of Grady's Famous Catfish Cakes . . . her new favorite Texas recipe!

Brooke Elizabeth Malouf

Brooke Elizabeth Malouf moved back to her native Dallas after taking graduate classes in Portugal. She began working on the book TEXAS MEN as a PR consultant—but soon found herself on the phones interviewing famous Texans, at photo shoots for Dot Com stars, in helicopters flying over ranches, and at her computer editing letters and profiles from sunrise to sunset. "Working on this book has been a million phone calls, a thousand faxes and a great privilege. I have met some of Texas' true heroes, who use their blessings to help others in need."

Brooke is a graduate of the University of Virginia and has her MBA from University of Dallas. She is working on several PR projects and finishing her first novel.

Brookscompany@hotmail.com

Ray Payne

As a fashion photographer, Ray had always dreamed of working in Paris, France. He finally got there and thought everything was right in the universe. But one night, as he sat in his Paris apartment drinking a bottle of wine and listening to Willie Nelson's *Star Dust* album, it hit him—there's no place like Texas! Raised in King Ranch country . . . Texas is home. It's where he'll stay.

Now based in Dallas, TX, Ray has had more than a few unique experiences shooting TEXAS MEN. His first Texas Man photoshoot was with race car driver Johnny Rutherford. The session began quietly enough, but by the end of the shoot Rutherford had the photographer and his crew rolling on the ground, laughing at his "Tall Texas Racing Tales"! Shooting Fort Worth preservationist Steve Murrin was another unforgettable experience. There they were, in the middle of the Fort Worth Stockyards, blocking traffic as Murrin posed beside a huge Longhorn! All the TEXAS MEN shoots were memorable, but Ray's son still talks about his personal favorite, with "Rollerblading Outlaw" Arlo Eisenberg, who gave him free rollerblading tips after the shoot!

www.rpayne.com

Fran Reisner

Fran Reisner, a National Award Winning Photographer who has an undeniable passion for the artistic beauty of her trade says, "This job was perfect for me because it offered new creative challenges and gave me a chance to meet some interesting Texas Men in the process. What I love about my business is capturing the essence of the individual and telling their story on film."

Although she was raised in the Pacific Northwest and was educated and started her family in California, she is glad to call Texas her home now. Says Reisner, "I feel a sense of energy and pride in Texas that I've not experienced anywhere else."

www.franreisner.com

Tauma Wiggins

During the TEXAS MEN book project many of the Texas Men grew familiar with the "tomahawk" phone calls, from Tauma, whose special assignment was retrieving their sometimes rather allusive profiles. "I've learned a lot about publishing from this project," Tauma says, and then adds, "but definitely a whole lot more about men!"

Raised in Austin, TX, "right down the road from a field a bluebonnets," Tauma went on to receive degrees at Texas A&M University and the Rice University Publishing Program. Tauma has plans to write books of her own, but in a slightly different genre then Texas men—children's literature.

Mikel Wixson

When he received news of a two-week photo assignment in Texas, his good friends told him he probably would never come back. "I'll be back in Los Angeles in no time at all," Mikel thought. Well, here it is four years later, and he's still in Texas! He loves the diversity of people here. It provides him with endless subjects for his camera, all the way from the flatlands of West Texas to TEXAS MEN.

One photo shoot that sticks in his mind was for Texas Man Clay Duncan, who attracted a lot of attention with his Texas good looks. The shoot had been difficult to schedule, so Mikel breathed a sigh of relief when everyone showed up. Five minutes later, he was staring at giant rain clouds looming overhead. True to Texas weather, the next minute, the sun suddenly came out, so they started the shoot. To make a long story short, everyone ended up completely soaked. However, all the ladies agree these shots are some of Mikel's best!

A Big Texas Thank You!

Kodak Professional

PHOTOGRAPHY CREDITS

PRINCIPAL TEXAS MEN PHOTOGRAPHY BY

Ray Payne: Cover and end sheets (engraved silver), cover (Martana nameplate), book jacket (leather chaps), 4, 8, 9, 14, 42, 50, 52, 54, 64, 78, 84, 90, 96, 110, 114, 118, 120, 122, 128, 138, 140, 150, 156, 168, 184 (Texas Men brand), back flap (Martana with yellow roses), back cover (Martana with Lone Star flag).

Fran Reisner: 26, 32, 34, 36, 38, 40, 62, 76, 132, 134, 154, 166, 188 (top right and bottom right), 189 (center), 190 (Stylle Read's mural), 192 (barn wood star).

Mikel Wixson: Cover (boots), 11, 12, 22, 24, 30, 44, 46, 48, 56, 68, 70, 72, 74, 82, 92, 100, 104, 106, 108, 112, 124, 126, 130, 146, 160, 172, 174, 176, 178, 185, 186, 188 (top left, center left and center right).

ADDITIONAL TEXAS MEN PHOTOGRAPHY BY

Walter Arce, Photo Courtesy of Interstate Batteries: 94.

Tony Baker, Photo Courtesy of MCA records: 158.

Charles William Bush, Photo Courtesy of Majlar Productions: 6.

Coco: 80.

Terry Colby: 148.

Jose Czabajszki: 88.

Bill Denver: 28.

Dennis Fagen: 52.

John Geider: 164.

John Glowczwski: 58, 66, 98, 144.

Carrell Grisby: 136.

J. Rene Guerrero: 162.

Ginger Hahn: 188 (bottom left).

Bader Howar: 102.

John Jefferson: 142.

Shelly Johnson: 189 (top).

Alberto Kerbow: 20, 86, 180.

Michael Manuel: 116.

Barney Nelson: 60.

Howard Pearlman: 189 (bottom).

Jay Presti: 170.

Opposite Page: Mural by Stylle Read

TEXAS

"From the outside looking in,
you can't understand it.
And from the inside looking out,
you can't explain it."

Joe White

Director, Kilgore Oil Museum